Hanratty on Karate
Training the Body and Mind

John Hanratty

DEEP STANCE MEDIA

Print Book ISBN 978-1-7380380-4-6
E-Book ISBN 978-1-7380380-5-3

Version 1.0

Cover design by Karolina Wudniak www.karolinawudniak.com
Illustrations by Enzo Amogan

With gratitude to

the senseis who shaped my journey

and the students who enriched it.

CONTENTS

INTRODUCTION

This book is a collection of my thoughts on the practice and philosophy of karate. I discuss how it can be used to develop the body and mind, what a lifetime of training has provided to me, and the benefits it has provided to the thousands of students I have taught over the years. It is part biographical, part philosophical, and part practical.

In these pages, I share what karate has meant to me as a lifelong pursuit and what I believe it can offer to others. That said, there is no "one karate." We each take different things from it and interpret its meaning in our own way. This is part of the richness of the tradition and complexity of karate. I am simply sharing my version of karate: Hanratty Karate, you could call it.

Although I discuss some techniques and training methods, this is not a how-to manual. For a detailed breakdown of karate techniques, you can refer to my book, *The Shotokan Instructor's Handbook*. Other excellent resources include *Karate: The Art of Empty Hand Fighting*, by Hidetaka Nishiyama and Richard Brown, the *Best Karate* series by Masatoshi Nakayama, and *The Complete Idiot's Guide to Karate*, by Randall Hassell and Edmond Otis.

The above books should be seen as a supplement to training, since any book is of limited use when it comes to physical instruction. The best way to train in any martial art is in a dojo under the guidance of an experienced instructor. And, of course, no technique should ever be used to harm another person except for the purpose of protecting the life and limb of yourself or others.

Karate training is not easy. You need a certain mindset to get into it. It is physically and mentally hard. But it is also physically and mentally healthy and rewarding. The whole thing about karate is, it is in the moment. You cannot think about much else when you are doing karate. The past is the answer and the future is the question. Right now is what you are doing.

CHAPTER ONE

EARLY YEARS

I grew up in the port city of Liverpool, England, in the years following World War II. You had to be a tough kid growing up there at that time. You played in bombsites, you threw bricks. Playgrounds were steel and wood and broken glass.

Other kids my age tended to be bigger. Many still are. I was small because of a wartime diet. But my spirit was always large. My wife once asked a childhood friend of mine, John Bate, what he remembered about me from school. He responded, "One thing I remember about John is that he was scared of nothing."

My hardest fight was just getting through life when I was younger. Liverpool was a very tough city. It was also one of the most cosmopolitan cities in England, with all sorts of nationalities. There was tribalism based on local and regional accents. Your accent reflected which city or region you were from.

I lived in Liverpool Eight, which was a particularly rough, working-class area with high unemployment. It was right down by the docks. You had to rob things off the docks just to feed yourself.

You tended to distrust anyone from outside your area. If you ventured outside, people wanted to know why. You were seen as disloyal. This kind of tribalism encouraged the formation of gangs. Almost every kid I knew was in a gang. We would throw stones at other gangs to get them out of our area. There was no shortage of stones because rubble was everywhere.

Regional loyalty meant you would never go to the authorities about anything, because everything was looked after within your own group. The last thing you would do is bring in the police because they did not come from your area. When I was a kid, I never knew anyone who was a police officer.

I was basically a war orphan. My mother abandoned me when I was an infant. I have no memories of her. My father spent several years in an Australian prison. Even when he was in England, he was not a presence in my life. I grew up with relatives or, more commonly, I was in foster care. As a foster child, I always felt that I was treated second-best to my various foster families' biological children. I also suspected my foster parents of fostering only so they could obtain government funding.

While Liverpool in those post-war years was a difficult place to grow up, it did not feel like hardship to me at the time. It was just the way things were. I rarely watched television or saw movies, so I had little exposure to other possibilities until I got older.

Life was full, despite the deprivations. You were thrown out of the house first thing in the morning and you did not return until it was dark. In those days, kids were not wanted in the house. You hung out with your mates and played games in the streets. I remember laughing as a kid, but I do not remember Christmas presents.

I was often angry as a child and young man. I would never back down from any kind of fight. In fact, sometimes I would probably go looking for it. This was not a good trait. It came out so that you did not get stepped on. You stepped first.

My anger probably came from my childhood environment, from the lack of family. It was certainly not nurturing. I was a product of the environment, and the environment was tenuous. You were always on the edge of going this way or that way.

The first school I attended, when I was four, was called Saint Malachy's Catholic Primary School. You had to sit there all day during your lessons, with your arms crossed, otherwise the "sister teachers" (nuns) would come around and hit you. My early school life was largely a battle waged with the nuns. Despite having no children of their own, they considered themselves experts on how children should be brought up. Any kid who doubted this would have the living crap beat out of them.

As part of the after-school activities, you could play football, you could box, you could do whatever you wanted. All the schools had different teams. You were allowed in the after-school boxing club, provided you were good enough. You could not box at four or five years old, but you were allowed to pound on the bags, skip rope, and watch the older kids training. They let you start training as you got older.

You would be wearing gloves but no helmet. You usually had bare feet or plimsolls (flat gym shoes, if you could afford them). The gloves were massive, battered old leather ones. They used to oil them up to cover the cracks in them. They tended to just throw you in with whomever. If there was a particularly skillful kid, you would be used as cannon fodder for them until you got better.

Due to my irregular home life, changing between foster homes in different parts of the city, I attended five or six different schools. Two of them had boxing teams. One was Sacred Heart Catholic Primary School, but they would not let me on the boxing team. They said it was full. I went across the road to a Church of England school called Harrison Jones. Their boxing team started at 4:30 p.m. I was 10 years old. I ended up fighting for them in the Liverpool Finals.

Boxing is a physical challenge and not much intelligence is required to overcome that challenge. But as you go on, you start to look in-depth at the techniques. If you are particularly interested, you will delve into the history and philosophy of whatever fighting art you are practicing.

On the boxing team you learned the various punches. There are only about six basic punches in boxing. You have a jab, a hook, an uppercut, a cross – not that many. Then you put those basic punches into various combinations. That is boxing. The rest of it is footwork, fitness, and timing.

I left school at age 15 to work on the pilot boats that ferried pilots to the ships near Liverpool. When I was 16, I joined the Merchant Navy, working as a galley boy, because of the security it offered. Your job was secure for the duration of the voyage, and there was a chance your position would be renewed when you got back. You received three meals a day, or as much as could eat, actually. You worked seven days a week, but you had free food and board.

The Merchant Navy gave me the amazing opportunity to see far-off places like Central America and the west coast of the United States. By age 18, I had circumnavigated the world.

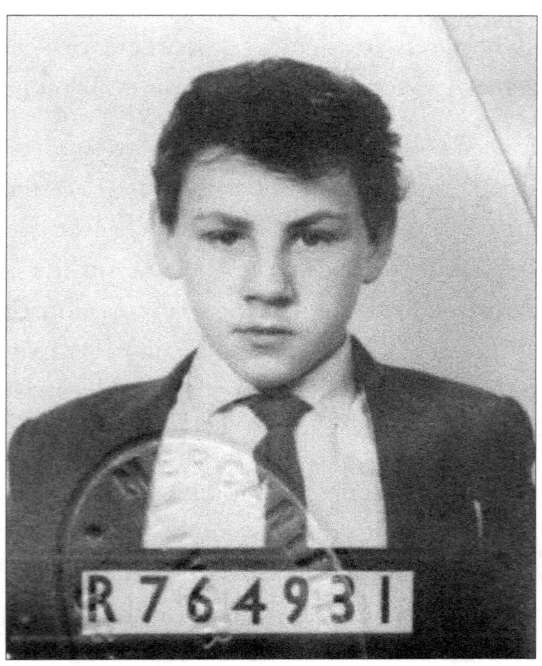

Me at age 16 in the Merchant Navy

The structure and organization on the ships was a comforting change. It was not exactly a family, but you were safe because you were fed and had a place to sleep. That was a big thing for me, because when I was in foster care, I had run away from home a few times and slept in hedges. The police would bring me back.

Although my childhood was marked by physical and emotional deprivation, I was intellectually enriched by books from an early age. I was an avid reader, conning my way into libraries. I got deep satisfaction out of educating myself about what else was out there in the world. I also did a great deal of reading in my years at sea, enough to realize the poor state of my formal education.

I looked at the Army as my next step, since enlisting would give me a chance at the education I had missed out on. With the traveling I had done, I probably knew more about the world than the average kid my age, or even many adults, but I wanted a real education. Something with which I could earn a living.

The Army provided this by first upgrading me to Basic GCE level (high school diploma). I was a willing learner and found I had an aptitude for technical subjects.

The Army put me with the Royal Armoured Corps, joining the First Tank Regiment in Germany. I learned all about engines and transmissions and learned to drive anything from a 65-ton tank to a Land Rover. I was like a duck in water. I also took extra night classes to upgrade my education, so I could get into university.

It was not all positive, though. I worked against authority in the Army. It seemed like they promoted the stupidest people just because they had been there longer or said, "Yes sir!" the loudest. The officer in charge often could not add two and two.

In karate, it was different. I accepted the structure because it was obvious that the instructor was better than me. In a dojo, the guy in front was clearly better than you and he was showing you how to get there as well.

CHAPTER TWO

KARATE ROOTS

My karate journey began in 1969. I was 25 years old, no longer in the Army, and working as a taxi driver (eventually owning a fleet of six taxis). Joining a karate club was a decision that would change my life.

The first club I joined was in Prescot, a town just east of Liverpool. It was run by Frank Vernon, a founder of the KUGB (Karate Union of Great Britain). When Frank's club lost its venue at a community centre, he suggested I join the Red Triangle, a famous Shotokan club in Liverpool.

I was hooked on karate from the start. I loved the discipline, the challenge, and the whole training regimen. Eventually, I was training twice a day and going to all the camps and seminars I could. If it is something you love, it is easy to do. I got a rush from achieving mastery over techniques. I was lucky to have stumbled on the best club and instructors one could hope for.

While life growing up was a challenge, karate was a challenge of my choosing. Once you accept that challenge and start into it, you do not want to back down. You will feel like a failure if you do.

I found that karate gave me everything – physically, intellectually, morally. I still take the philosophy to heart. The philosophy, of course, is not to knock seven bells out of everybody, but to try and be a better person.

Nowadays, almost nobody asks people why they want to study karate. They just go, "Okay, here's your class, this is how much it costs." If you ask a new student, "Why do you want to do karate?"

they often do not know. Or they have a false idea of karate from TV or movies, or maybe they have joined only because their friends joined.

This is a difference from when I started and why I did it, compared to modern day. I looked at it as an amazing way to stay fit and a great challenge. I thought, "Okay, this is what I want to do." I had no long-term goal in mind; I was just going to do it. I did not worry about grades. I did not know what happened when you got to black belt. That all came as a surprise.

Before I ever stepped into a boxing ring or karate class, I had learned lessons in the streets about fighting, particularly as a taxi driver in Liverpool. It was a very quiet week if I did not get into at least one fight.

Most of all, I had learned to go hard and to go fast, and to hit the other guy first. You had to be absolutely determined, with no thought for consequences. These days, people think about consequences before they act, because it is ingrained in them at school. When you are in a fight, you cannot think of the consequences. You want to get out of it as quick as you can, and brutality is the way you do it.

Violence is actually a way of communicating. It may be a primitive way of communicating, but you certainly get your message across really quick.

What set me apart as a fighter was probably the competitive side of me. I have always been competitive. I play golf these days, and I get pissed off when somebody beats me. My wife, Julie, beats me all the time, but I still go at it.

It is a very personal thing with golf because you are always playing against the course. It is like karate. Most of the time, you are not going against anybody else. You are simply trying to better yourself. I mean, you can go into competitions, but competitions are rule-bound. Street fights, on the other hand, are not rule-bound. On the street, anything goes.

Fear of the consequences gets many people hurt. Because most people do not have a fear of losing; they have a fear of winning. And that fear of winning is, "If I hit him, what's he going to do back to me?" I have never had that fear.

I believe that karate provided me with an outlet for buried emotions. I could not punch the crap out of authority figures such as my foster parents or the nuns at school, so I did karate. I loved the freedom. I loved the way it took my mind off everything else. When the instructor is telling you, "Do this, do this, do this," nothing else can get into your mind. If it does, you are probably going to trip over yourself or get punched in the mouth.

Every time I trained, I seemed to gain more control over my emotions. But it took a long time. It took me eight years to earn my black belt and I failed every single grading up until black belt. I failed each time but then passed on my next try. And a couple of times I half-passed, or got a B grade, so I had to grade again.

I was not too concerned about how quickly I got ahead. I just loved the feeling of being in the dojo and not having to think about anything else. I could just concentrate on getting my body to do what I wanted it to do. I got an awful lot from that.

As I progressed in karate, I started to calm down. I still love going to the dojo. I am at my very best when I am in a dojo. I am in the best state of mind. I can usually shrug off injuries. And I feel like I am doing something that I am good at, or that I want to be good at. If you strongly want to excel at something, you will eventually get there if you do the work.

When I started training, I did not have a definite goal. I just wanted to get better. I had what is referred to as "ambiguity tolerance." My only goal was to be as good as the people ahead of me.

You find ambiguity tolerance in many top-performing athletes. It could also be a businessperson, a scientist, or whomever. You know you will achieve something, without knowing how you will get there or even what the exact goal is. I had that mindset when I first started, though I did not know it at the time. I had no clue about *kyu* grades and how you got to them. When I got my Shodan (first-degree black belt) certificate, I almost fell over; I had no idea I would receive a signed certificate from the JKA (Japan Karate Association).

All I was interested in was training. I just wanted to go as far as I could. I could not see the end. It is like life. You live life without knowing what the end will be like or how soon it will arrive. You need that high tolerance for ambiguity. It is grit. It is perseverance. You do not know what you will achieve, you are just going to do your best.

Everything was hard for me in my early years of karate training, but my attitude was that I was just going to go at it. My attitude could have been better at the time, however. I still had my angry attitude from childhood. If I had calmed down and taken it in more, rather than trying to kill everything and overpower every move I made, it probably would have been easier on my body. Also, I would have had more control and improved my techniques more quickly.

Relying too much on aggressiveness in my initial years of training likely held me back. Karate was an anger release for me. So far as I was concerned, the world had treated me wrong. I needed an outlet for those feelings.

If you grow up in a harsh environment, you either learn to live with it or you do not make it. There are different ways of living with it. You can use it to make you better and get ahead in life and maybe even change that environment, or you can be the same as all the other idiots in that harsh environment and probably not survive as long as you should.

I always thought, even up to age 18 or 20, that I would be dead by 40. My feeling was, "I don't even want to live past 40 because your brain cells all start disappearing after 25 and your body is going downhill." It is like the line from an old song: "Hope I die before I get old." I believe now that my feelings were immature. They were probably an excuse for the lack of success I expected to achieve.

Ironically, when I was about 40, I was probably the strongest and fastest I ever was. I was even fighting in competitions until I was 50. Now, in my late 70s, I cannot do many of the same things, but I am still actively teaching, working out at the gym, and training in the dojo.

How you respond to a harsh environment comes back to Darwin's theory of evolution. People have different understandings of survival of the fittest. But it goes deep in people. There is an instinctive drive in your lizard brain: you want to survive. How you survive and remain at peace with yourself is up to you. I have managed to do it quite well. Some people can manage to do so without ever getting into a confrontation, but that is usually because of the society and culture around them.

If you live in a society where hardship is the norm, you must fight to get ahead or even just to survive. If you have come up a hard way, and people tell me I did, you get used to doing whatever is necessary. I never looked around for anybody to help me. That is the last thing I would do.

Over time, I have become adept at not reacting in a kneejerk way to other people's words and actions. As you get older, it becomes easier. When I was younger, certainly not. I would be in your face. My approach has evolved.

Everything evolves. It is natural to think evolution means progress, but that is not true regarding many things. Look at air travel. Fifty years ago, you were served delicious meals with fine China and sterling silver cutlery. Now, we are treated like cattle. It is similar with karate.

Many are losing sight of karate's purpose, what we are trying to achieve with it. Some will say, "We're learning to kill with one blow." What a load of bull. It is easy to kill with one blow: just buy a gun. That is not why you do karate. You do it to build the *budo* (martial) spirit, or certain aspects of it, mainly because it is satisfying on many personal levels.

I trained a lot during my first years in the dojo. After I earned my black belt, I trained even more. The constant input from training is what built the muscle memory, the technique, the power, and the speed, right up until my body started to let me down as I aged.

As you are training, you are analyzing everything you are doing and looking for more efficient ways to do it. Your body will tell you the most efficient way, but you often must go the long way before you find the shorter way. I tell my students: "If I go to your house and you say, 'Do you want a cup of coffee? Get me a cup,' it will take me five minutes to find where you keep the cups. The next time I am there, I might remember where it was and go straight to it. It is familiarity. Eventually, I will get the cup without even looking."

That is muscle memory and that is efficiency. Muscle memory builds in efficiency, hopefully without damaging you, if you do it correctly. That is how I try to teach techniques – the most efficient way possible.

There are three basic components to karate training. There are the basics, which we call *kihon*, where you learn each individual technique and what is behind it and how to do it. There is *kata*, which is the form, where you learn how to put techniques together in sequence (Shotokan has 27 *kata*). And then, of course, we have the partner work or sparring, called *kumite*, which involves applying your techniques and your timing.

My philosophy of training is based on my personal experiences, instructors I have had, and books I have read. I adopt the best examples and ditch the worst. My philosophy of life leans towards stoicism and pragmatism. This fits well into the karate mindset: doing what you can to get the best out of every day.

I have always enjoyed reading philosophical books. As you get older, your thirst for knowledge does not drop, or at least mine has not. If anything, it has gotten stronger. If something interests me and I do not understand it, I will research it until I do.

I had the same approach as a kid. For example, when I was a teenager, I was employed on an old tramp steamer (merchant ship) that had a triple-expansion steam engine. I was not trained in mechanics yet; I was just trying to earn a living. The engine fascinated me. I hounded the chief engineer until he made a drawing showing how it worked. (Steam is expanded in three stages in cylinders of increasing diameter to accommodate the steam's decreasing pressure and increasing volume.) My inquisitive nature served me well in my later career as a hydraulics engineer.

To understand me, you need to know where I came from. It is the same with karate. If you want to truly understand it, you need to know how it came about, where its roots are. The history of karate always interested me. You can go back thousands of years, probably to India, and follow *Bodhidharma*, who spread Buddhism as well as martial arts in his journeys.

Martial arts and religion have always had a relationship. You can look at the Shaolin monks, and the code of the samurai, *bushido*. A corollary is the Knights Templar in the Catholic faith and the Crusades. These are all martial arts. Look at knights and chivalry.

It is the same; nothing new. They follow paths through the world. Chivalry was the same as *bushido*, but the knights did not go around chopping up peasants just because they failed to bow.

If you are going to focus only on karate's history, that goes back to the late 1800s. Author Patrick McCarthy has probably done the most in-depth study of karate's history, but he studies all of karate, not just Shotokan. I only ever practiced Shotokan, so I tend to follow that line back, and Shotokan diverges from karate only in the late 1940s. Before that it was not Shotokan, it was just karate.

In my view, there are three general kinds of karate: Okinawan, Japanese, and westernized sport karate. There are distinct differences between Okinawan karate and Japanese karate, and the westernization of karate, as reflected in sport karate.

The original Okinawan karate was not supposed to be a style, but obviously it was, because different families trained in their own way and focused on certain techniques. There were also different styles based on geography, such as *Naha-te* and *Shuri-te*, named after the cities in which they originated.

Karate-do is a way of life. My karate is traditional Japanese karate. That said, I have nothing against sport karate. It is healthy, it is a recreational activity, and I love watching it. I have officiated it and competed in it.

I am sometimes asked how Shotokan karate differs from other styles of martial arts. To be honest, it does not. There really is no style, though it is hard to avoid using the term. Styles are primarily a western concept.

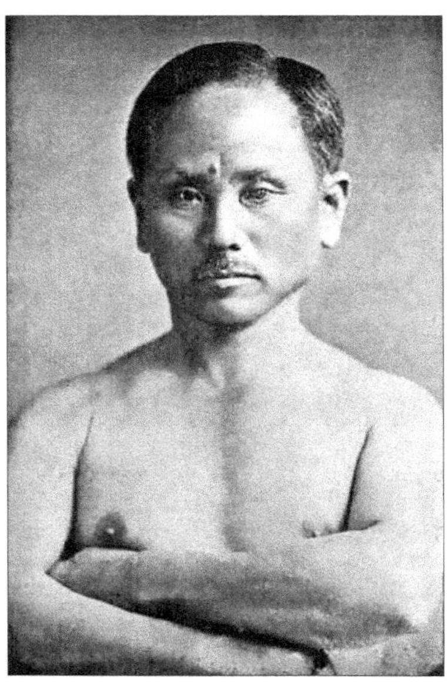

"Shotokan" was based on the name given to its founder, Gichin Funakoshi, a schoolteacher from Okinawa. "Shoto" means pine waves, which is how he signed his calligraphy and his poems. It was like a pen name. "Kan" just means training hall, so Shotokan means "The hall where Shoto trains."

Throughout his life, Funakoshi devoted himself to the study of karate. He originally named his martial art using the term "Chinese hands" (where "Kara" means "Chinese" and "Te" means "hands"). Subsequently, he changed the first character to signify "empty," even though it was pronounced identically. As a result, "karate" came to be understood as "empty hands." This modification severed the links to Chinese origins and aided in the martial art gaining acceptance in Japan, particularly during a period marked by strong nationalistic sentiments.

Funakoshi understood that to gain complete acceptance within the martial arts community, karate needed to align with the principles and philosophical base of traditional Japanese martial arts. These foundational beliefs are encapsulated in *bushido*, which directly means "military-knight-ways" but is more widely recognized as "The Way of the Warrior."

Bushido represents the comprehensive moral code of the ancient samurai class. It balanced the freedoms of power with the responsibilities of a protector, and also instilled in samurai a fearless and honourable approach to facing death.

When karate was imported to Japan from Okinawa, people tended to base the styles on which *kata* people did, but if you see a *kumite* match, you do not know what style they are. If somebody comes along and hits you in the mouth, you could not say "Oh, that was a Goju-ryu guy" or "That was a Shito-ryu guy."

There were no grades or titles when Master Funakoshi left Okinawa in the early 1920s to teach in Japan. A system that clarified the hierarchy was adopted to fit the Japanese culture, which put great emphasis on status and hierarchy. The *dan* and *kyu* grades were suggested by Kanō Jigorō, the founder of Judo.

When you look at the original Okinawan techniques, there were no high kicks. That changed in the late 1940s, mostly because of

Gigō Funakoshi, Master Funakoshi's third son, who brought in high kicks and other innovations. High kicks were traditionally avoided because they are dangerous: they expose your groin to attack and are inherently unstable. High kicks were introduced because low kicks to the groin were penalized in competitions. Some say that high kicks were inspired by Savate (French kickboxing), which actually takes its kicks from ballet.

High kicks are not efficient. They are not practical for self-defence or close-quarter combat, especially if you cannot pick your location. Unless you have complete surprise on your side, high kicks do not generally work.

Back stances, which involve putting your weight primarily on your back leg, are also unique to Shotokan. Back stances are entirely different in other styles.

To me, the *katas* are what differentiate one style from another, more than anything else. If you take a basic *kata* such as *Bassai-dai/Bassai-sho*, there are probably 15 variations on it. That is what separates the styles – not so much what we do, but how we do it.

The application (*bunkai*) of a movement in a *kata* is unique to the person doing it. The way I apply a certain technique is going to be different from someone with a different body type. The technique may be the same, but the application could be very different.

Above the entrance to our dojo is this maxim of mine:

Kata without ego.

Form follows function.

Some people do not see that. They would rather make it like a dance. *Kata* needs to work. This is why I am not a fan of *kata* competitions. They only show the absolute surface. Also, I do not understand why they differentiate men's and women's *kata*, since they are just dancing. No reason they cannot dance together.

Karate organizations in Japan date back only to 1948, when various university clubs formed the JKA. Master Funakoshi, though regarded as the father of modern karate, never had an official position in the organization. His role was as a figurehead and a source of inspiration rather than an administrative or official one. He focused on promoting karate as a martial art and a way of life.

The JKA faced a crisis in 1987, following the death of Masatoshi Nakayama, a key figure in the organization and a prominent student of Gichin Funakoshi. The leadership vacuum following Nakayama's death spurred internal disputes and led to the organization splitting into different factions. This fragmentation challenged the JKA's unity and raised questions about the future direction of its teaching methodologies and philosophies.

With Masatoshi Nakayama in Vancouver, British Columbia, in 1986

The differences between karate organizations, even among those that purport to teach traditional Shotokan, highlights the individuality of karate training. It is another illustration of how there is no "one karate."

20

Unfortunately, many karate clubs are purely commercial. This takes away from the true spirit of what we are teaching. Our organization, the Canadian Shotokan Karate Association (CSKA), is basically run as a nonprofit. Our focus is on maintaining our teaching standards, not on making money. If you are going to teach it right, the way it should be done, the training will never be easy. This might limit our membership somewhat, but I have always focused on the quality of my students rather than the quantity.

Traditional karate, the way I look at it, should not be ego based. You should always have humility because you can never achieve perfection. Humility is particularly challenging for someone who is very assertive, as I am. It is just my personality.

If you took the great masters, such as Enoeda, Shirai, or Kanazawa, and had them all do the same *kata* – totally different. How they performed the techniques, what they put into it, their mindset – totally different. Everybody does it differently. If you had everybody in the world sing the same song, even in the same key, same notes, each person would do it their own way. It is the same with karate. It is unique to each person.

Someone might say, "I do JKA karate." No, you do not. You do your version of it. We are all different. You would need the same DNA to do a technique exactly the same as someone else.

Japanese practitioners say they added the *bushido* spirit to Okinawan karate, meaning it improves your character. I believe it does do that. I believe karate improved me, and I believe it has improved a lot of other people. Whether they trained with me for a month, a year, or 30 years, hopefully I gave them something that influenced their character development and impacted their life in some way.

Karate is a very complete art. Aikido says, "We do all throws" and Taekwondo goes, "We do all kicks." In a karate dojo, we do it all.

We can do a class on throws, we can do a class on kicks, we can do a class on joint manipulation. It is a complete system. All the other styles are trying to do the same thing. Sometimes we go off to this side or to that side, but we are all going down the same road.

It does not matter which style you study. If you study anything long enough, you will be good at it. There is no such thing as anybody being cleverer or better than anybody else. It is just that you are more experienced in that field than the other person.

It is a deliberate choice on my part to study only Shotokan karate. I believe in the value of deep, concentrated learning in one area rather than a broader, more superficial approach across multiple disciplines. This depth of study allows for comprehensive understanding and mastery.

This approach is based on the principle of inductive learning, which involves deriving general principles from specific observations or experiences. With a martial art such as Shotokan karate, this means learning and understanding broader concepts of the art through the practice and mastery of specific techniques, *katas*, and principles. I believe this approach is more rewarding and enriching, allowing for a profound grasp of the subject matter.

CHAPTER THREE

INSTRUCTION

My club is not the easiest club to train in because we are quite strict. The training is rather regimented, arduous, and rigorous. You must be fit to do it, so part of the training is gaining the fitness and flexibility to do it. I look at someone joining the club as putting their trust in me to get them fit, show them techniques that will not damage their bodies, and give them the confidence and self-esteem they seek.

What I teach, and the way I have lived, does not fully fit in today's world. But then again, traditional karate does not fully fit. It fits in this world as a recreation, as a fallback, as a means of gaining confidence, as a way to build resilience. Karate builds leadership qualities and gives you purpose. Once you have conquered a certain amount of training, you can apply those traits outside the dojo. The discipline you gain is easily transferable to your work ethic and other parts of life.

You learn the techniques, you learn the values, you learn the morality that is involved. There is an authority figure that you submit to. Whether you like authority or not, you must accept it. There is a lot expected of you and a lot expected of me. What is expected of me is that I keep the discipline. You are expected to submit to that discipline and to do as you are told so you can learn the correct way.

Shuhari is a Japanese *term* for the stages of learning, from beginner to master. In the first stage, you do exactly as you are told, as you learn the basics. It is like being an apprentice. The second stage is self-exploration, where you play around with it and make it work for you, but you hold onto the values the lessons are based on. The third stage involves taking everything you have learned, all you have explored, all you have developed, and passing it on. But you must pass it on correctly, which I try to do.

Walking into a dojo for the first time can be intimidating. Whenever we get a new student, I say, "This is so-and-so – introduce yourselves later." If you are going to a dojo for the first time, you might be looked at a bit for the first half-hour or so, but most people there, especially if they are senior, have been in your position and want to help you along and make it comfortable. We want to share what we know and feel about the art.

With beginners, I rarely see the attitude I had. I knew almost straightaway, "I love this; I want to do it." When a kid walks into the dojo, you can often tell whether they will stick with it. You can see if they are interested and can see the potential of pushing ahead.

Most people who join a martial arts club know very little about the different styles or techniques. What is most important when choosing a club is finding an instructor you trust. Your first relationship is with the instructor. If you do not trust them, it does not matter how good the style is, you are not going to train. The first person you see is the instructor. He or she has a big responsibility.

Unfortunately, not all instructors are worthy of your trust. Many are just out to make money or stroke their own egos. I have never done that with my club. As I have always told people, we offer "traditional training for serious students."

I discovered my forte was not in fighting, not in competing – it was in instructing. I honestly think I am not a bad instructor. I can get people to do stuff, I can get them to do it right, and I have turned out many good people. There are also people who have quit because they disliked the way I do it, but that is okay. You are always going to get that, even if you are doing it perfectly. Some people just want to be babied.

I teach in the manner of my original senseis, Andy Sherry and Keinosuke Enoeda, who were very authoritarian. To me, that is the traditional Japanese style. When you are a sensei, which just means someone who has gone before, the roles are very defined. There is the student's role, which is to learn, while my role as an instructor is to show you how to learn. Not what to learn, but *how* to learn. Because everybody does it differently.

I use micro and macro cycles when I am teaching. A macro cycle will take a period of three to four months to cover a particular concept. I may not cover it every class, but I will come back to it every two or three classes. A micro cycle is what I want to cover in three classes, or about a week's worth of classes.

What gives me the most satisfaction is when I am explaining something on the floor and I see lightbulb moments where the students get it. It happens a lot, especially with the advanced grades. Suddenly, what they have been doing in basics just clicks. It is like getting the exact right gear in a car – clunk!

We have a big guy in our club – he is 6'4" and probably 250 lbs. He is a powerlifter, so he tends to think his strength will get him everything. He has been with the dojo for several years and his techniques have started to improve. What is not always improving is his mindset, because when he goes faster his mind takes over and his technique goes out the window.

There is a fine line between chaos and control. As an instructor, when you want somebody to control their technique, the best way is to tire them out. I hit them with a load of basic cardio techniques that will sap their strength. When that happens, they cannot be mad. It is very hard to be mad when everything hurts and your muscles are gone and you have no breath in your body.

Your emotions come down to the same level as your body. At that point I can do something with you. Now I can show you how to be more efficient and to utilize whatever energy remains to make a technique. Because bad techniques are inefficient. They use much more energy than a correct technique.

Efficiency equates to speed. When you are looking for power, one of the components is acceleration. Force is mass times acceleration. You cannot get that speed if you are angry. Well, you might be fast, but your muscles are going to be off. You will not have the right rhythm. You will be going the long way around with your punches – you will be throwing haymakers, which is not the most direct way to the target. Your fine motor skills go out the window, due to the adrenaline rush and due to fatigue. As a result, it will be easy for someone who knows what they are doing to throw you or to do a joint manipulation.

I often tell my students, "I'm not here to show you what I can do, but what you can do, and you can be great." People do not know how good they can be. My job is to bring that out. It is not about showing them what I can do. These days, I cannot do an awful lot. I mean, what I do will work for me, but I need my students to push themselves. I teach them to take great pride and a sense of achievement in the techniques that they master or simply improve.

My teaching method is designed to get the best possible results. People say I am a tough instructor. If I were not as hard on students, I would not get the same results. I am not screaming at you to get your respect. I am not particularly interested in your respect, so long as you get what I am teaching you. That is my driving force: to see that you are doing it right.

I have always been very conscious of whether I am doing techniques correctly, because teaching is also learning. I have been learning all the years I have been teaching, and I am still learning how to get people to do everything correctly. Hopefully, over time, they will discover what works and use a little innovation to make it even better.

It is all about interpretation. Everyone interprets life differently. It is the same with karate. Interpretation is everything. Some people are built particularly well for it. But it is like beauty: a beautiful technique is only skin deep. What matters is whether it works.

Practice does not make perfect; practice makes permanent. Therefore, you need to practice your techniques correctly, otherwise you are just making a bad technique permanent. If an instructor does not tell students they are doing it incorrectly, they do not know.

Some people think it is wrong to correct others. The person being corrected might think they are being criticized. Criticism often equates to failure, particularly in Western countries. However, there is a difference between criticizing and correcting. It is a fine line, I admit, because you obviously must critique them to correct them, but in no way is it a failure. You must look at what is behind the critique. The intention, for me, has always been to make the student better.

I have had the privilege to teach thousands of students at seminars all over the world. I enjoy meeting karate instructors and students. It is very satisfying when you visit a club that is at a decent level and you can move into some advanced techniques and philosophy. On the other hand, if you find a club that is not quite up to your usual standard, it is satisfying to bring them along and show them where they are going wrong.

When you travel a long way to teach a seminar, you can feel like a bit of a celebrity, with the spotlight on you, but I always think that is fake. I always feel like it does not apply to me. I go out and teach the class with the thought, "Okay, this is just like a class I'm teaching back home."

I often do not know what I am going to teach, especially if I go to a seminar and they are suddenly like, "Take the class." Sometimes you think, "This is going to be easy, they're going to enjoy this," and three moves in, you find they are all over the place. That is when you must quickly change the lesson to match their level.

I am probably a dying breed in that I insist on details being correct. If they are not correct, I will correct you. If you take it as criticism, then you are looking at it from the wrong aspect. It is mostly correction, not criticism. A lot of clubs have a big fear of correcting or criticizing a student who is lazy or slow because they might lose their monthly fee. We do not worry about that. With the way we have set our club up, it is more or less self-sustaining. We are always on the edge financially, but it is satisfying that we have been going so long, despite that.

The hierarchy in a dojo is obvious as soon as you enter. The instructor has his own area for changing and administrative tasks, and the Dan grades (black belts) stake out their area. The pecking order becomes clear. This reflects the *kōhai/senpai* dynamic with the Japanese. There is always a pecking order, and *kōhai/senpai* just means junior/senior. At the end of the class when we recite the *dojo kun*, I always say *kōhai*, which means "junior student" and that student is referred to as *senpai* by those of lower rank.

The dojo is not a democracy. This may come as a shock to some who enter a dojo for the first time. As a student, you do not get a say. I do not encourage people to question what I am teaching, unless I ask something, and mostly all I will ask is, "Do you understand this? Does this make sense to you?" If it does not, I will try to explain it better.

Often, I have entered the dojo with a theme or sequence in my mind thinking, "This should be easy. We'll go over this and lead into something else with it," but then I get stuck on the first step because what I thought was easy, almost nobody in the class can grasp. At that point, you must take a step back and show how you arrived at what you were thinking. Explaining your methodology is a little tiring at times. It is much better if they can just grasp the technique physically and then hopefully bring the mental side in afterward.

As you get older, you learn that being judgmental is an ego-based thing. I try to keep ego out of the equation when I am teaching karate. When long-time instructors give themselves titles such as "master" or "grandmaster," I see that as pure ego.

Some people, even white belts, come onto the floor and look down the line and think they are better than the other students. That is a good way to think, perhaps, but keep it to yourself. Be happy with yourself because you are better. Do not put the other guy down because of it.

When I am teaching seminars, and this is probably a fault of mine, I tend to cram in more than the students can absorb. As a result, I have the reputation of giving very hard classes. They go, "Oh God, it's Hanratty. We'll be beating the crap out of each other." Because I always put people together straight away, to see if a technique or sequence works, and there is no opportunity for daydreaming or dozing off. If you are face-to-face with someone, you better be in that moment and paying attention or you will get punched in the mouth. I tell the students, "This is what you do, and this is what it's for – now make it work."

I have had some awkward students. You can teach them the same thing a hundred times and they still get it wrong, but you learn to look for little signs of progress. When you point that out to them, they start to feel better about themselves.

At my stage in life, my focus is on motivating others and continually innovating the techniques and practices I engage in. Given the ever-changing nature of our bodies, each day presents a new challenge. What was effortless at 25 becomes a formidable task in your late 70s, but I strive to adapt my movements to achieve the desired results.

I was exposed to difficult training from the start. It was always challenging. The way we were taught in the UK was very different from most clubs today. It was even stricter and much harsher, even than my current dojo. I think we had two women at the Red Triangle, but they did not tend to stick. In fact, there were often no women and there were no kids under 14 until they started a special children's class. I used to teach the children's class and some of them became champions. I was quite pleased with that.

I had an even stricter style when I first started teaching. My classes were also more repetitive. Repetition develops muscle memory; it gets the neural path embedded. That is basically the way I was taught. I have since figured out why I was taught that way. It was because they did not fully understand what was behind it. As I became capable of performing techniques, I thought, "I don't have to do this 45 times." Why not? Because I know the physiology behind it, and I know the mindset that fires the physiology.

Once I have taught a particular technique to a student, my priority is to get their mindset right. This is a much harder job than getting their kick straight. I want to get more into their mind because, frankly, the chances of you ever having to use a technique in a real confrontation is very low. Some people tell me they have never been in a fight in their life.

I do not go easy on any student. I am the same with everybody. I am as consistent as possible, and you cannot be consistent if you treat somebody different. I am very good friends with one of my students and I shout at him like hell.

If somebody is good, I will go harder at them to be better. If I am shouting at you, it is not that I am criticizing you, nor am I just being mean to you. It is that I know you can do better. I am aware of your capabilities, and I think you can make more of your ability. Many people do not understand the difference between ability and capability. If I think you are capable of more, then I want more. That is why I push you.

The way I teach, I do not deliberately go out of my way to make it hard. I try to get you to control your mind and your body. Your mind is a very, very fine tool if used correctly. Anybody with any intelligence or academic background knows you must be disciplined to study. Karate involves studying your own body and making it work the way you want it to work. This is hard for many people because your body is naturally lazy. It resists exertion. Your muscles are weak. Your joints will hurt. That is just the way it is. You need to gain control over your body.

You can tell if a particular student is not focused on what they are doing. You can see that their mind is elsewhere. They bring their problems in, even though it means they cannot perform as well.

The best motivational teacher I ever had was Sensei Enoeda. He was on fire with karate. Pure motivation and enthusiasm, with amazing technique and charisma. When he walked in, everybody stopped and looked. He carried himself so well. That was my inspiration. I thought, "I want to do that. When I go in there, I want people to say, 'Yeah, this is going to be a good session, we're going to learn something, this guy is going to motivate me.'"

The best technical teacher I ever trained under was Sensei Hidetaka Nishiyama. He could explain how to coordinate the body and produce the most power from every movement and every technique.

The last few years, because I have lost much of my flexibility and mobility, I have started basing some of my teaching on Nishiyama's methods. He explained in detail exactly how your body works and how to get the most power out of it so that you make a finishing blow. A lot of the technical details I learned from Nishiyama went into *The Shotokan Instructor's Handbook* that I published in 2020. My methods are probably UK-style, but the methodology of the curriculum is probably more Nishiyama.

Hidetaka Nishiyama visiting Calgary, Alberta in 1987

Our club has always been accused of training too hard. That is something I cannot stop doing. My overwhelming desire is to teach karate the way I believe to be right. After 50-plus years, I think I know the right way to teach a technique. I will not let you do something incorrectly.

Many instructors are like, "Oh, his foot's a little out of place, that doesn't matter." You will constantly hear me saying, "Get your stances deeper, get your feet straight, get your back straight." I am always correcting. Again, I do not say criticizing, I say correcting.

I tell my students, "If I'm not correcting you, it's because I don't think you're interested enough, so I'm not interested in helping you. If I'm shouting at you, if I'm constantly correcting you, then obviously I think there's something more there that we can bring out. I haven't given up on you."

Instructors such as Sensei Enoeda did not think anything of sweeping your leg out from under you if you were wrong. Same thing with Terry O'Neill. I remember one of my first classes at the Red Triangle. We were doing *Heian Shodan* for maybe the tenth or twelfth time, sweat is dripping off me. I get to the *age-uki* (upward block) with the *kiai* (shout) and I wipe the sweat out of my eye. Next thing I know, I get swept onto the floor. O'Neill says, "That's not in the *kata*."

The student has a defined role in the dojo and the teacher has a defined role. Your role as a student is to pay attention, absorb everything you can, and do what the instructor is asking you to do to the best of your ability. The instructor's job is to explain it so there is no misunderstanding and to make sure you do the technique to the best of your ability, while keeping the safety of other students in mind.

I want to bring you along as best I can. Some people respond well to me shouting at them while others respond to me patting them on the back, which I very rarely do. If you are doing well, I will say, "That was good," and then I will leave you alone. But if you are not doing it right, especially if I think you might hurt yourself, I will correct you.

For example, it is easy to put too much pressure on your ACL (anterior cruciate ligament) when your foot position is wrong. Some people try to kick too high, so they have an unstable base. It is going to hurt them, not me. I tell them they need to pivot on their support foot when they do *mawashi-geri*, or they are going to rip everything up on the way down.

There is a reason we do things the way we do. Generally, the aim is to deliver a technique with power and precision, with the least amount of damage to yourself. When you get into a fight, you want to get out of it as quickly as possible. You want to be able to go home and say, "You should see the other guy." More than likely, you are going to get hit, but the idea is you can deal with it.

Some people have never been hit in their lives. They come into a dojo and getting hit is a massive shock to them. Or they have never been shouted at. I like to use my voice. *Kakegoe*, which is based on the use of voice and shouts in Japanese music and kabuki theatre, involves using your voice as a weapon. I use it just as much when I am teaching as when I am fighting. Instead of hitting you with a stick, I hit you with my voice.

Some of the phrases I use in class are original to me, and some are from my previous instructors. Everything is an imitation of something else, anyway. There is nothing new in the world. You paraphrase it, you put it in your own words.

I think it all comes from how you understand it. Your interpretation might initially differ from your instructor's, or it could evolve uniquely, as everyone approaches karate in their own way. The karate I do is Shotokan, but it is *my* Shotokan.

If someone said they did Hanratty Karate, hopefully they would be thinking for themselves. They would certainly have very good basics. I can spot a student of mine from years ago. If a student comes back after 10 and 12 years, their basics are solid. Their attitude is also good. Also, the way they fulfill the drill they are doing, their awareness, is strong.

Spatial awareness, knowing what is happening around you, is very important. This is especially true if you are facing multiple opponents. You must be particularly aware of which way you will move and which opponent you will take out first.

Anybody who has been training for 40 or 50 years, whatever style they train in, has learned something from it and are a master at what they do. If you study any subject that long, you will be an expert in it. When you are a true expert in anything, you can spot the flaws in your own system, you can spot the flaws in your own character, and hopefully you can paper over them and they are not too obvious.

Here is a summary of the primary mental objectives that karateka should aim for:

- Demonstrate a continuously robust spirit;
- Maintain *zanshin* (focused attention);
- Engage in training earnestly and persistently;
- Practice self-control;
- Keep emotions balanced;
- Show respect for fellow students and instructors;
- Aim for thorough mastery of techniques, rather than a broad but shallow approach; and
- Remember that the ultimate aim of training is self-betterment, not merely competing with others. Training is its own reward.

CHAPTER FOUR

STRENGTH

When I was training at the Red Triangle in Liverpool in my late 20s, I did some weightlifting as a bit of a supplement. I wanted to build up my body because you used to get the crap beat out of you by the big guys. You were fighting the likes of Frank Brennan, Terry O'Neill, Bobby Poynton, Billy Crystal. These were strong men with amazing techniques. We would have lineups all the time (facing a line of opponents, one after the other, until the instructor said stop), or just spar for an hour.

I lifted weights to bulk up, to get some power behind the punches. I was fast enough, but I needed some strength. I used to work out in an old-fashioned gym that lacked machines, where all the weights were homemade. It did me good and I put on a bit of muscle. When I went to Canada, in fact, one of the guys I trained with asked me to enter a bodybuilding competition. I said no. I am not into that stuff.

Even when I was training six days a week, I would do a bit of weightlifting. I used to do a boot camp which involved circuit training and had a lot of weights in it. When I was getting a team ready for a competition, I would go to the dojo at 5:30 a.m. and lead a session before work. We would do a fair amount of weights, particularly resistance training.

I was not obsessed with fitness so much as I was obsessed with training, because I wanted to be the best I could be at karate. Actually, I was not even interested in being the best. I was interested in having the people I was training be the best. I would take my students to a competition and people would say, "You guys train too hard, you take this too seriously." And I would think, "How stupid! How are you supposed to take it?"

I still go to the gym a lot, and I love it. It is a great feeling. Exercise releases endorphins, of course. Karate does that too, but it does more than that, because it teaches you at the same time. It is not just lifting weights or riding a bike. My usual routine is to go 40 or 45 minutes on the bike to get cardio going. Then I get on the weights and do my sets.

Occasionally I will start mentally drifting off while I am doing cooldowns. I cannot do that in karate. In karate, I am trying to get everything right, making sure everything is lined up, that everything is in the right position. Everything is involved in my core and goes out from my core.

It is different when you are doing weights or exercise in the gym. If you are doing flies, all you are thinking about is flies. You can probably look at the ceiling and count the cracks. But if you are doing blocks in the dojo, everything is involved. Your whole body and your whole mind are involved in that one action, so nothing else can come in. It might be mindless, but that is the whole idea. Mindless is not a bad state.

For some people, karate comes too easily, so they soon pack it in. This means they have not been challenged enough. I always found karate a challenge. It did not come easy to me at all. I had to see the mechanics behind it, the physiology.

I reference everything towards the mechanical aspect, whereas a lot of people focus more on the philosophical side. They will endlessly analyze one move to make it fit some ideal image. "This is the way it should be." No, that is the way *you* think it should be, but if you go back to the source, they are not really concerned about how perfect the move looks, they are more concerned with how it works.

I have always focused on how techniques work because I could not make them perfect and beautiful. Eventually, I could almost go into full splits, I could kick people in the head, and I could do jumping kicks, but I always had to work, work, work for it. Never forget, making it look good does not make it work, does not make it applicable. What makes it applicable is how you employ it.

There are days when you hit a plateau and think you cannot go further, and that is when I will come along and make you go further. That is my job, really. But it is also psychological. You are going to feel good about yourself when you come out of class, especially if it has been a really hard class, where you are dripping sweat and your legs are aching. You come off the floor and you think, "There's not many other people that can do that."

I always said that to myself when I had an especially hard session at one of the Japanese dojos or in the UK, where you practically crawl off the floor. You look at the other guys and they are all slumped over, with barely the strength to get in the shower. You tell yourself, "Well, not many people could do that, could they?" That is a good feeling. It is not just pride. It is earned pride.

Just like with any physical activity, such as skiing or riding a bike or whatever, there is a risk of injury with karate. But the risk of injury in a properly run karate club is actually very low, because everyone is being careful. It is what we call "controlled violence."

When you apply techniques with another student, I want you to bring out the best in your partner. This requires you to do your best, so that you both try. If one person does not try, the other person does not have to try. We should push our partners to get the best out of them. This also brings out the best in you.

The people who stick with karate tend to be dedicated people. They work hard at what they do and they worked hard over a period of many years to get where they are. There are many people who think they are so-called karate masters but are actually rubbish. Mind you, I do not look on myself as anything special in karate. I just did what was necessary to get better at it. I think anybody who has done it for a few decades knows what they are talking about and deserves the respect they get. I doubt you can last 40 years as a charlatan running a McDojo.

With young kids, you can usually figure out in the first class whether they want to be there or if it is their parents' idea. If you can interest the child, it does not matter about the parent. But these days, you often see very young children being pushed into it, like, "You're gonna do karate, or baseball, or hockey." I do not look on karate as that kind of recreation. It is not playtime.

I am not just training the body. Most often, students do not give up because their body gives out – it is their mind. If your mind is weak, there is no way you will survive a confrontation where you need to be strong. Your mind is what counts. The aim is developing the strength of mind to defend yourself or to get yourself out of a situation.

Most people succumb to verbal abuse more than physical abuse, particularly females. You want to build the mental part up, so you are like, "I'm not going to take that; I know how to punch – bang!" And away you go. "Sensei has put me through a lot worse than this – I'm not going to take it from this guy!"

A lazy student, where they just won't try, makes me angry. Not that they cannot do something, but that they won't. If you get someone who won't, there is not an awful lot you can do.

It can be extremely difficult with many young kids. I hate to say it, but many kids these days are lazy. They have sat on their couch and played games and they get dragged out and told to do some kind of activity. They are brought to the dojo, where there is a disciplined atmosphere. They cannot talk. They must stand still. They must do exactly as they are told, so they do not like it.

Usually, it is the parents who push their kid into doing karate. To me, this is failure transference. They cannot motivate their kid, so they want the instructor to do it. You do occasionally get the little jewels who take up the challenge and push themselves. We have a few that still hang around. We have brought them up from six or seven years old. Some have become national and international champions. They are the ones you look for.

You can see signs right away that they might be the kind to stick with it. Enthusiasm, especially in a child, is hard to hide. You will know all about it. If they are reluctant, you will know all about that too. Not many young children have poker faces.

When teaching kids, it is important to break up what you are teaching so you do not bore them. For example, we have a Little Tigers class for kids aged five and six, which I personally do not teach very often, but sometimes I go in there. I will spend no more than five to seven minutes on a technique before I change it. Hopefully they retain some of what I tell them.

If you spend more than 10 minutes on one technique, young kids get bored. They have done it to the best of their ability and will not try anymore. You must keep changing it and then coming back to it, or make it into an enactment of some kind, so they can treat it as a game. Kids love to compete, so if you can get them competing with it, that will engage them.

There is a great saying, and I am not sure which old master said it (they would probably all claim credit): "Man does not make the art; art makes the man." This is particularly true about karate. It is something you must keep going. As we always say, "The water stops boiling once you remove the heat." That is why we want you to keep training all the time. It is going to be more satisfying. The hardest part about karate is getting out your front door. After that, it is just really enjoyable.

To fully develop your potential in karate, or in any endeavour, it takes a lot of time and dedication. What do I get out of it? I get the satisfaction of knowing that what I am doing is, to the best of my ability, the right way to do it.

I do not care what your ability is. What I am looking at is your capability – I will help you achieve that. It may take a long time or a short time. I have had white belts come in and they have performed great techniques within half an hour. But that is just one technique. Now I have a few thousand others to work on with you. Just one technique is not going to do it.

Most of the time, there is nobody in front of you, just your own limitations, just your body and your mind. And that is probably 80 per cent of the training, because you must learn the techniques and you must learn to apply the techniques in sequence.

I look on karate as a lifetime experience. The philosophy I have is, you dedicate yourself to one activity that you love in your life. If it makes you money, you are very, very lucky. If it does not make you money, you still do that activity because you love it.

I feel good as soon as I am on the dojo floor. I may be in pain, and I have had loads of surgical procedures, but when I put on my *gi*, and step onto the floor, I feel good.

I am sometimes asked what made me stick with karate if my first club was so strict and demanding. It probably had a lot to do with coming from that very rough, tough background in Liverpool. We did not have the luxury of being offended at anything. Life was offensive, and you just had to deal with it.

Everything you do is a challenge in such an environment. You just get used to it. Defeating the challenge becomes an enjoyable thing. You almost become addicted to the adrenaline or the fact that you can do it when people say you cannot. Basically, it is a form of stubbornness.

It is like anything else in life – if you set out with goals and you achieve those goals, the sense of achievement promotes a great feeling inside of you. Then you set and achieve more goals and more goals. After fifty-odd years of training, maybe I am making a bit of progress. Regardless of how true that is, I am not stopping.

Some have suggested there was something unusual about me because, as a young man, I pursued extra challenges during the post-war hardships in Liverpool. I am reluctant to think I am different from anybody else. Life is all about choices. You are the choices you make. There are so many forks in the road. When you get to my age, and you look back on them, you see so many times when you could have gone a different way.

Most successful people have experienced hardship. They have had some tempering in their life, like a piece of steel that has been molded. If you are soft as putty in your early years, you will probably be soft as putty in your older years. But there comes a time when you get through it, and this is my belief: when you get to a certain stage in your training, where it is very much a part of you, you are going to be as good as you will get, but you can apply what you have learned throughout life. Your philosophy becomes based in what you do and who you are.

Resilience is often described as the ability to return to what you were. Resilience, in my mind, is not returning to your previous state, like releasing a stretched elastic band. The kind of resilience to which I aspire is to improve on my previous situation.

Resilience is the ability to adapt, and I do not mean adapt to change, because obviously I can adapt to change. I have changed countries three or four times. Rather, it is to adapt your thinking. If you can adapt your thinking to someone else's point of view, somebody who points out something new to you, this gets rid of a lot of ego. If you can deal with your ego, you can deal with anything, whereas people are usually their own worst enemies. They start a self-belief that becomes dominant, and they bury it under stubbornness. If you can adapt to changes in your life, that will be to your advantage.

CHAPTER FIVE

CONFIDENCE

You gain a certain bearing and self-assurance after many years of karate training. Years ago, I was doing a magazine interview after winning a tournament in California. The interviewer said, "You're a 250-pound mouth on a 150-pound body."

There is no question that karate will give you self-confidence. I will not say it gives you mastery over your body, necessarily, but it certainly gives you a lot of confidence, knowing you have these techniques in your bag. And you are going to look at people's opinions from the perspective of what you know and have experienced.

I have always been confident teaching because you must teach what you know. And what I know, I know because I have practiced it over and over and over and over. I know why I am doing it and I want you to learn why you are doing it. If you know your subject, you are usually confident.

Although I am confident in what I am teaching, I sometimes feel lack of confidence regarding, "How can I make this person understand what I'm teaching?" So, it is more of a communication issue on my part. I am not particularly glib. My vocabulary does not flow as much as I want it to at times.

Sometimes parents will come into the dojo and say, "I think my kid's getting bullied and I want them to be a lot more self-confident." The thing is, it is very hard to teach somebody self-confidence if they are only at the dojo an hour or two per week.

Self-confidence comes from your environment around you, especially at home, and it comes from within.

Telling people to be more confident by standing up straight and projecting themselves does not always work. If you get a shy or weak person who thinks they are not good enough to stand up to a bully, that is very, very hard to change in a couple of weekly sessions. What is needed are changes at home, where the parents can influence the child, because self-confidence comes primarily from the parents.

Over the years, I have seen some sad situations. Parents have brought in a child who was rather broken. I cannot change that, at least not in the short term. It is like taking them to school and saying, "He's never been any good at math – teach him." It is hard to do that from scratch.

When I teach self-defence, the first thing I emphasize is posture. Good posture and a positive outlook make a big difference. This does not mean staring at people. Just glance at them, meet them in the eye, and carry on. Avoid facial expressions. Even smiling could be offensive or provocative to some people. Just look at them and carry on with your business. Try not to look down at the ground after you glance at them.

Predators look for prey. They look for those who appear vulnerable. Do not be prey. That is the opportunity aspect of avoiding danger. You can decrease the opportunity with your posture, your attitude, and your general body language.

Body language is extremely important. I am a short, fat, little old guy. But I have body language that tells you otherwise. Some people say that 80 per cent of communication is body language. I am not sure it is that much, but it is certainly a lot.

Regardless of what image karate and other martial arts have with some people, for most people it is about personal development. Most people who practice karate do it to feel good about themselves. It is not what you can do or what potential you have – it is how good you feel and what it does for you mentally. It makes you feel good inside. It gives you good self-discipline. It gives you confidence that carries over into all areas of your life.

CHAPTER SIX

BREATH & VOICE

Right from the start, I teach students to breathe properly. I tell them to relax the abdomen and to let the diaphragm drop so you can fill your lungs as much as possible. Then you tense the abdomen to push the diaphragm up, to empty your lungs as much as you can. Try not to use your shoulders. This is a nice, slow method of breathing that really oxygenates your blood.

You can also use this method, especially the tensing of the abdomen and the diaphragm, when you are making *kime*, or focus, on your techniques. It helps you connect your main body mass to your technique, so you have more force behind it.

The other kind of breathing would be more reflective of your body rhythm, how you move. When I am fighting, my breathing pattern is adapted to my movements. As I advance, I breathe shallowly to mask from my opponent any discernible rhythm. Conversely, when I retreat, I inhale deeply to rejuvenate before re-engaging. Additionally, the employment of rhythmic, pulsating breaths – characterized by a series of quick "huh" sounds – helps to create a dynamic motion in my abdomen. This abdominal movement creates moments of vulnerability, known as *kyo* (a state of being unprepared or off-guard, physically or mentally), which occur between each technique. Understanding this is crucial; if you inhale at an inopportune moment and are struck by your opponent, you are likely to get winded.

I teach students to make a correct *kiai* with as much volume and force as you can. Instead of thinking, "Oh, everybody's looking at me because I'm making a noise," I make the most noise there. I do not care if people look at me. There is psychology behind it.

The function of *kiai* is to coordinate the breathing with the movement. Your technique and your breathing should finish together. It should bring your technique and your spirit and your body together. It helps you focus your mind. A *kiai* can also be used prior to delivering a technique to elicit a flinch or freeze response from your opponent, or to deflect attention.

When we do bag work, if someone has a habit of holding their breath, they soon have nothing left in the tank. I have them do three loud *kiais*, and it is amazing how it reoxygenates the blood. Also, when we do partner work, I make sure the students *kiai* when they counterattack.

When working with a partner or an opponent, many variables are involved. Psychological variables are probably the most important. You can use all sorts of weapons, but probably the most powerful weapon is your voice.

In any kind of confrontation, more people submit to verbal abuse than to physical abuse. They will give in just because the other person is so loud and overbearing. It is like a big dog barking at you. This is used all over the world. Police forces scream their heads off: "Freeze!" Then there are battle cries. This is the use of the voice as a weapon. I try to encourage that.

Over time, students feel less self-conscious when they make a shout or a loud noise. Most people are shy and reluctant to make a loud noise. They would rather not be noticed. But if you can get them making those noises, get them vocalizing and asking questions, they will progress a lot faster.

A couple of years ago, I was on a train with my stepdaughter and her daughter, and a bunch of rowdy teenagers got on, swearing and carrying on. I shouted "HEY!" Then I quietly said, "Behave yourselves – there are kids here." And they just shut up. It was an effective way of controlling the situation. I was giving them a taste of my dojo voice.

Regarding the use of your voice when instructing, you must project so students can hear you. In a small dojo like mine, it is not much of an issue. But if you are teaching in a large dojo or at a seminar in front of 150 or 200 people, you must project.

Raising the volume of your voice is all part of the rhythm of breathing. However, you cannot talk as you are doing a technique. For example, if I am doing a side thrust kick, I cannot talk during that. I must breathe out and push my body with the technique.

I want you to see how I am doing it, so I explain it first, then I do it, then I explain what steps I went through to achieve what I did, and then I have you to try to do it. You will not do it identically, but I want you to understand how your muscles are going to work, what messages you need to send from your brain, and I use my voice to communicate this. Your repetition of the technique builds your muscle memory.

Where I got the reputation of being harsh was that immediately when someone went wrong, I would shout, "Stop! You're doing it wrong!" And they go, "Well, he's a jerk. He's always screaming at us." But I am sorry, I cannot teach "wrong." And I will not accept "half good." It has got to be there. In my dojo, you will do it until you get it right.

CHAPTER SEVEN

DEFENCE

Master Funakoshi's famous maxim "There is no first strike in karate" is a noble sentiment. It emphasizes the fact that karate is for the protection of life and limb. It should never be used to bully anyone or to harm the innocent.

It takes some explaining, perhaps, to square this sentiment with my philosophy, which has always been, "Attack the intention." If somebody intends to harm you, you are within your rights to stop them. You stop it the quickest and most brutal way you can.

Nobody is going to attack you unless they think they are going to win. And what you must do straightaway is break that attitude. Break the idea that they are going to win and that they are going to win easily. You cannot do much about a person's motive for attacking you, but you can dissuade them, straightaway, of the idea that they are going to win.

It is like a burglar going into a house: the last thing he wants to do is get caught. If he thinks he will get caught, he will not go in there. It is the same with people who are going to attack you. I am not going to get attacked by someone who is four feet tall and weighs 100 pounds, because that person is unlikely to think they can win.

Many people these days have second thoughts when it comes to defending. When I say you have to attack the intention, you must go in with the idea that you will kick this guy in the head or sweep his legs out from under him or knock him out. That is your first thought.

If you have a second thought, such as, "I might get charged for this," or other consequences, you will not do the first action, and you have lost. When you defend yourself, you must defend yourself outright. You cannot think about anything else. Otherwise, you may lose the chance to defend yourself.

With self-defence, you must deliver the very best technique you have, when you need it. You must be at your very best at the instant you need it. Most people cannot. Their mindset stops them. If I am in a self-defence situation, I am going to throw my very best punch, my most lethal technique, and walk away.

When I am teaching self-defence classes, I tell my students to bear in mind what they can control and what they cannot. I tell them to consider three factors: location, opportunity, and motive. Two of them, you can control.

Regarding location, you can choose not to go down dark alleys at night or to put yourself in a bad situation where you are surrounded by idiots, like a bar. As for opportunity, stay alert. Stick with a group. Stay in a crowd. Most people will not attack if there is a crowd.

The only thing you have no control over is what motivates the other person. Their motive does not matter. All that matters is what they do.

Most people who commit an offensive act – an assault or a robbery or whatever – do not think they will get caught or get their lights punched out. They think they will get away with it. If you take away the opportunity and the location, you diminish the factor of, "I'm going to win, I'm going to get away with it" by a big amount. Also, they do not expect you to fight back. If you smack them or disable them in some way, they will be the one on the defensive.

Random, unprovoked attacks are particularly tough to deal with. Fortunately, those people usually do not have particularly effective techniques, so you get a chance to perhaps cover yourself, particularly if you have trained enough that you instinctively cover or move, rather than flinch and freeze.

Rather than an ineffective reflex, such as a flinch, we want a trained reflex. A response is often too slow. A response generally comes after perception. You perceive something and you respond to it, while a reflex is an automatic response. You may not consciously perceive what is happening, but you react to it. We are looking to make your reflex a technique. When you train enough, it becomes automatic.

That said, I do not generally teach students to make automatic blocks. Typically, when you block, it is because you perceived an attack, so it is a response. I would rather have you attack as a reflex. That is the response I am looking for. Your technique would be to attack their intention.

Your blocks are the start of using that reflex, because most of your blocks start from a defensive position. If you get attacked in the head, your hands go in front of your face, and you expand from there.

With *age-uki* (upward rising block), your hands should be crossed in front of your face before you do the block. You see many schools where they just bring their arms straight up, which does not block anything. It is useless. They are looking only at the end of the technique, but you should be making this defence all the way through the technique.

The only reason you ever block is to counter. If you had a chance to get away, you would. You do not block as a defensive mechanism. You block to counterattack. You block to open your opponent to a counter technique. Yes, you are stopping someone from hitting you, but if you knew they were going to hit you, why be there?

Most of the time, people train in the dojo against a single technique. I soon have my students dealing with double attacks, and I want them to get in their counterattack between the two techniques, when their opponent is *kyo*, or open. People are open when they start a technique or between a technique. That is why you go in, you do not go back. You do not flinch.

You must get rid of that flinch response. A flinch response is actually a learned technique. If you suddenly move your hand toward a baby, the baby will just keep looking at you. As it gets older, it starts to flinch. It is not entirely instinctive.

Most people will tell you what they plan to do. They get themselves worked up to do it. The hardest thing to defend against is an unprovoked attack out of nowhere. The way a person works themselves up to attack is connected to a concept called the monkey dance.

In 1967, Desmond Morris released a bestselling book called *The Naked Ape*, which is still in print. It goes into the psychology of people's behaviour and how it relates to animals. There are strong similarities. People who want to intimidate you puff out their chest, spread their arms wide, try to make themselves bigger. They do not exactly beat their chest like gorillas, but they start to strut around. It is obvious.

You see it with belligerent drunks. They start to push their way around. They start to pose questions like, "Who are you looking at?" There is no obvious answer to that, so you know where that is going. He has taken one more step from the posturing to the verbal. It is a step up the aggression ladder. Only he knows how many steps he is going to take up the ladder. You are quite entitled to take that ladder away from him anytime you want, because there is obviously a threat.

The best way to deal with someone like that, obviously, is to just walk away. If you cannot do that, or you have someone with you who may be in danger, you are dutybound to protect that person, particularly if they are a woman or child. And that is where you make your decision. If there is an intention there, attack it. I have done so in a number of situations.

Timing in a confrontation is very difficult to teach. We have three basic timings. The Japanese analyze the timings to death: *sen-no-sen* (before timing, or "attack the initiative"), *tai-no-sen* (simultaneous block and counter), and *go-no-sen* (block and then counter). It makes sense to focus on timing. It is extremely important.

Go-no-sen is not really used in boxing because the emphasis is not on blocking and then counterattacking, but on avoiding getting hit in the first place. In boxing, "blocking" typically means just covering up and waiting for an opportunity. Boxers are trained to "roll with a punch," using it to their advantage. For instance, if an opponent throws a left cross, a boxer will roll with it while simultaneously delivering a right hook, taking advantage of the opponent's position.

In contrast, karate employs a different approach, often focusing on the idea of blocking attacks with the belief of, "I know how to block, so I won't get hit." However, this mindset is unrealistic. It is like a boxer entering the ring under the illusion that they will not get punched. Every boxer knows that taking punches is an inevitable part of a match. If you go into a street fight thinking you will not get hit, you are wrong. You are going to get hit.

Some people have natural timing, and timing is rhythm. Everything in life has a rhythm. Once you pick up a rhythm, you can pick the spots you want to act upon. It is really hard because you must control a lot of emotions when you are fighting, to pick up a rhythm. Sparring in a competition, generally, is all about attack. It is not really about defence. At least, that is what I teach. Attack is also what a street fight is about.

I do not care what all the street fighting and self-defence books say. In the vast majority of fights, the first strike determines the outcome, particularly if you know how to deliver the technique. You are going to put the guy on the ground right now. And if you do not, you are going to follow up immediately with three, four, five more strikes. You do not wait to see if the first strike worked.

You cannot go into a street fight thinking, "I'll wait until he moves and then I'll block him." Because 80 per cent of fights are finished with the first blow. If you get your first punch in, if you get a good technique in, that is going to be good enough. Like Mike Tyson once said, "Everyone's got a plan until they get punched in the mouth." Getting punched drastically changes your mental outlook. There is nothing worse than getting your nose broken.

I once got my nose broken in the first round of a boxing match. (My current nose is my third remodel.) All they did back then was stuff it up with tissue and you continued boxing. I was only 10 or 11 years old at the time and I finished three rounds. I won, but I was not happy about it. Getting hit like that made me furious. The reaction I have to pain is to try and kill the person.

Everyone talks about opponents as if you are facing each other in a mutually consensual confrontation. That is not always the case. In fact, it is usually not mutually agreeable. If you are in a sane state of mind, you do not want people to attack you.

Fortunately, there are almost always signs that people want to attack. You need to identify those signs. It is very hard to do that if you get into a state of anger or fear. These emotions are often brought about by verbal confrontation, to start with. If you can make someone angry, verbally, then you can probably beat them, provided you are not angry yourself.

You cannot let the other person's emotions infect you. There is an old saying to the effect of, "You're wasting your time using reason with someone who didn't use reason in their argument." You are much better off having a discussion than an argument. Discussions resolve things. Arguments mostly escalate them.

Mizu no kokoro is often translated as "mind like water." It is a beautiful image. If you have a very busy mind, you should keep your body still, and ready, and relaxed. And if your body is moving quickly here and there, your mind should calm down and look for opportunities. If your mind and body are both fast, you cannot look for opportunities – your focus is out the window. If both are slow, you are probably asleep.

You should bring your mental state almost to the opposite of your physical state. You also need to counterbalance your opponent's state. If they are in a high energy state, you need to calm down. Slow down and watch what is happening.

When we are doing distance training, I like to get students close to each other. This is hard because psychological variables come into play. People do not like to be in other people's space. I tell students, "You should take up your opponent's space. Make them uncomfortable."

Imagine you are riding home on an empty bus late at night. The last thing you want is for someone to get on the bus and sit next to you. They would be invading your space. You are going to be acutely uncomfortable. A lot of scallywags realize this. They will deliberately provoke people by entering their space. Guys who want to intimidate women will stand very close to them; it is a form of bullying and a form of abuse. It is also a way of intimidating and overcoming your opponent. Your voice can come into play as well.

CHAPTER EIGHT

OFFENCE

Many acts of violence are cultural, just as the various martial arts are rooted in different cultures. This means you will probably depend on certain techniques more than others, depending on your culture. In England, for example, they use a lot of headbutts. When I use a headbutt – and it is my go-to for an initial attack if I am close enough – I can do it straight on or I can do a whipping action. (A whipping action actually causes a lot more damage).

Some people use only hands. Some Chinese styles use a lot of hands. The closed fist came a little later. It comes from boxing. In the Greek Olympic games, they started to use a closed fist.

Knee strikes come more from Muay Thai. We use them in karate, in quite a few *katas*, but they are not used to great effect. You also do not see many knee drops, though if you sweep someone, one of the best things you can do is drop on them with your knee.

Patrick McArthy estimates there are 36 Habitual Acts of Physical Violence (HAPV). These 36 actions represent the most common forms of physical aggression a person might encounter. The actions include various forms of strikes, holds, locks, and other techniques.

Karate certainly opened up a myriad of ways for me to put my opinion across in a street fight. It gave me many more weapons. Before karate, I had never considered using my elbows much.

With street fights in Liverpool, you would throw as many headbutts and punches as you could, and maybe the odd knee if you could find a target, but guys are very adept at protecting their genitals. It is an instinctive thing, so you do not always get it in, but you might take them by surprise. With karate, I found I could get in close and use my elbows. They do a tremendous amount of damage.

Before training in karate, I had never considered using straight finger strikes, but they are so effective. It is all down to target: for eyes or throat, they are great. Anywhere else, you will probably break your fingers.

If you do not use the *makiwara* (a stiff vertical board with padding), you probably rarely make a correct punch. You probably have a bent wrist. Therefore, every so often, I bring out the heavy bag for students to work on. This is also why we do push-ups on our fists. It encourages a straight wrist and toughens up the first two knuckles, which we strike with when we punch.

If somebody has a weapon and you do not, you are at a big disadvantage, no matter how much you train. One time, in my taxi driver days, a guy slashed my chest with a knife, which made me really, really angry. I broke his wrist with a ratchet bar that I kept in my car. He dropped the knife. Then I swept him and smashed his knee. I took his knife and kept it in my toolbox for years. It was a pretty good knife.

It is especially dangerous if someone who is unprovoked comes at you with a weapon and you do not know they have a weapon. If that happens, you are in big trouble, no matter who you are. Same if they manage to hit you with a sucker punch. Big trouble. It used to be like that in Liverpool. There were a lot of unprovoked attacks. Face slashing with a box cutter, crazy things like that.

There are a lot of silly videos online showing how to supposedly defend against a knife or gun attack. They almost always presuppose that you can see the weapon. But this is often not the case. If a guy has a gun, do you think he will show it to you? He will probably just take it out and shoot you. Also, an attacker is unlikely to strike you just one time. He is going to do multiple attacks. And if they have a knife, they will probably aim for bleeder spots, which roughly correspond to pressure points. Bad news.

When you are attacked with a weapon, you need another weapon, if at all possible. One time, a guy attacked me with a long screwdriver. I was able to nullify that by going straight inside and kneeing him as hard as I could in the crotch and jamming my fist in his throat at the same time. He went down like a sack of flour. If somebody has a knife or other weapon, run away or look for an equal or better weapon.

Forget the other person's action; attack the intention. Because action always beats reaction. You should always look for the most effective way of putting your opponent out of commission.

When I look at karate, I focus on the original point of view: besides the philosophical, it is about self-defence. The most effective way to defend yourself is to deter your attacker by zeroing in on vulnerable targets, and the best targets are vision, breathing, and balance.

If an opponent cannot see you, they cannot hit you. Therefore, if you can, go first for their vision. I will do this more often than not: go straight for the eyes. But you must get in close to do it. To get in there, you can open them up with certain basic techniques. If you get their vision, they are done. They are absolutely done.

If you cannot get the eyes, go for the breathing. I generally go for the throat with a straight finger strike. If I cannot get that, I can usually pick out someone's solar plexus without a problem. Or a palm strike to the nose. Basically, any peripheral nervous system, where the nervous system is close to the surface.

Then, if nothing else is open, go for their balance. Throw them on the ground so you can run away or can finish them. But do not go to the ground with them. Kick them in the head or drop your knee on them.

The above scenarios are based on the assumption that you have good reason to believe you or someone else is in serious danger of harm and you are unable to remove yourself (or them) from the situation.

I get a lot of enjoyment out of any technique or combination that I can explain and show, and clearly works. I take something from a *kata* and boom! It works. I do not struggle with it. It is just smooth as hell, and even the person I am working with goes, "Wow, that worked well." That gives me a lot of satisfaction. However, keep in mind that applications and even drills are only "What if?" situations.

There are only a few techniques I can do by example these days. I used to demonstrate everything. I would go, "This is how you do a *mawashi-geri.*" "Ooh, that's so high, so strong." But now, I need to tell you how *you* can do it. Again, my aim is to show you how good you can be. That is my whole job. The only question is, how good do you want to be, and how much do you want it?

What comes only with a lot of experience is applying your techniques with different people. Judging distance *(maai)* is hard, which is why I always go in close. Learning control is hard, too. You get to know your exact control. You learn how to throw a full-power punch and stop it just on target. That comes with practice.

Learning correct distance and timing is extremely hard. They are the hardest concepts to teach. It is much easier to teach students that every kick starts with your knee raised, for example. Some people have natural timing – they can pick the right time to go in and move out. Others never get it.

One attribute that all successful athletes have in common is speed. It is the key to success in martial arts and most other athletic pursuits. We acquire speed through practice and repetition. Familiarity increases efficiency, and increased efficiency allows for increased speed. At the same time, being fast is not helpful unless it is combined with proper timing and distance.

Suppose there are several guys threatening me. Which one do I attack first? The biggest? The smallest? There is an exercise I used to do. I turned my back on three students. They chose which one would attack me. When I turned back around, 95 per cent of the time I would attack the one they had chosen. It is about reading the body language. You attack the one that is going to come at you first. You take out the most imminent threat.

If you are lucky and have perfect genes, you get a karate champion like Frank Brennan. He came along and just overtook everybody because he had a body that was built for it and the right mindset.

Brennan was one of the best fighters I have ever seen. I was fortunate to have the chance to train with him for quite a few years. His absolute dedication set him apart. He was also big and strong and extremely fast.

Brennan trained every single day, twice a day. I was also training twice a day at one point. At the Red Triangle, you had to be invited to the morning sessions, which went from 10 a.m. to noon. If you just turned up, they would say, "What do you want?"

Brennan would go into full splits, no problem. But it did not come naturally. When he was a kid, he would put his foot on the banister at home and slide his foot up. He kept doing it until he got the way he wanted to be. He was one of the most flexible people I have ever seen, and one of the fastest and most powerful. He would train every morning and would also attend two classes each evening: the beginner class and the advanced class. At age 14, he was already on the British team. His kicking techniques were amazing, but he could also punch the lights out of you.

As for a streetfighter, the best I have seen was a Goju-ryu practitioner named Gary Spiers. I used to weightlift with him. He was a real gentleman if he was a friend, but he could also take on five guys and wipe the floor with them. And five guys in Liverpool is more than five guys in most other places.

Frank Vernon, my first instructor, used to say, "Never show an opponent your weaknesses." Never let them see if you were injured. It is about keeping a mental edge over your opponent. You can use psychology against an opponent as much as you can use physical techniques. I learned a lot about this topic from Sun Tzu's *Art of War*, which I first read as a teenager.

When I moved to Canada in 1980, I was put on the Alberta provincial team right away. At my first competition, I am slated to fight a guy from British Columbia. Someone tells me, "This guy is really good." I watch him fighting and he is quite fast.

Before our match, he goes into the washroom, and I follow him. He uses the washroom, washes his hands, and goes out. Just as he gets to the door, with a crowd of people around, I go, "You're supposed to wash your hands when you've been in the washroom." He turned around, and I could see I had got him. I had gotten into his head.

What gets me through a lot of situations is that I have a strong spirit, or sheer bloody-mindedness. I have gotten my nose broken in a fight and finished the other guy completely. If you have ever had your nose broken, you know it is not pleasant. It really throws your mind to hell. Pain is a stimulant to me. It makes me angry. If I get hurt, I get angry, and I tend to move faster.

A technique that I developed to a high degree was a double punch: I would do *kizami* (jab with lead hand), shift my back foot toward my front foot, then do *gyaku-zuki* (reverse punch). I could put that in almost anytime I wanted. I had a lot of power in it. Bang, bang! And you are down.

I could kick quite well into my 50s. But it was more of an afterthought. I would chase the guy with punches and then throw a kick. Or I would time it so I would go one, two, stop. Then, as he came back toward me, I would catch him with a kick.

Kime, or focus, generally involves tensing all your muscles at the moment of contact. You use *kime* to stop the technique. It should be as short as possible. When you hit something with a hammer, you do not hold the hammer there.

Some instructors say, in almost mystical terms, that *kime* generates power. They think *kime* is a transfer of force, that the quicker you make *kime* the more energy you transfer, which is ludicrous. *Kime* simply stops the technique.

The only reason you make *kime* is to create a break. It stops your muscles and then you move to another technique. And your target is not the person's chin. It is six inches past their chin (or other body part). It is like when you hit a golf ball or a baseball. You do not stop at the point of contact. You go past the point of contact.

I once attended a seminar where the instructor said *kime* involves transmitting kinetic energy. He said if he did a kick alongside a person's head, even if it did not contact them, it would knock them down. I said, "Can you show me?" He goes, "Well, I don't want to knock you down." I said, "I don't think you will. Can you show me?" He did not like that. Did not want to do it at all.

I have good control. I can go full power and stop my punch right on your chin. Your head does not snap. Without contact, there is no power.

We use *kime* in a few different ways. When you are focusing your power, you can do it fast or you can do it slow. You can do it on an extension or on a retraction.

With a thrusting technique, such as a front thrust kick, you use *kime* to stop the movement on the extension of the technique. You can also use it on a snapping technique, such as *uraken* (backfist strike), but you would be using it on the retraction of the technique.

Another type of *kime* that I have identified, which some people disagree with, is a long one where you are simultaneously doing a pushing and pulling, where you are tensing your muscles all the way through the technique. This is also a kind of focus because you must focus all your power into that movement.

This kind of focus may not be obvious in application, but it should be obvious in *kata* where there are slow movements – you should apply that tension to show how much power you are putting into it. It is like if you get grabbed around the neck and you bring your hands up to block and then you push down. You obviously have resistance that you must overcome, and this requires *kime.*

When making *kime* with a snapping action, there is no resistance; same when making *kime* with a thrusting action. There should be no resistance during the movement. The only resistance is when you hit the target.

If you are doing a thrusting technique, you are generally using rotation or momentum to provide power. You can use a snapping technique while you are in motion; you do not have to stop your momentum. Power generation is about coordinating the body in such a way that the rhythm brings everything together.

Over the years, I attended a number of instructor courses taught by Sensei Nishiyama, who had a unique way of teaching. He was not interested in the applications of *kata*, or even the applications in *kumite*. He was only interested in how to develop maximum power in each technique.

The sources of power that Nishiyama identified are:

- rotation or spinning
- vibration
- momentum
- pendulum
- lifting and dropping

Teaching people to throw is hard because they think it is about strength. It is not strength – it is just technique, it is how you turn.

Throwing comes down to physics: center of gravity and line of gravity. If you can get their center of gravity outside their line of gravity, you can get them down. It is not particularly hard, but you must think about it and work it out.

The only reason you block is so you can deliver a counterattack, and it better be instantaneous, because the other guy is not open for long. He is *kyo*, which means off. There are only certain instances where your opponent is off, where you can catch him.

When you are looking at *kyo*, your perception must be synced to an action. You cannot look and think, "Oh, there's an opening," and then attack. The opportunity is typically gone by that point.

Perceiving and then responding is what we do when we block and counter. It is one instance of *kyo*: between techniques.

Another instance of *kyo* is when your opponent is just deciding to come at you. I may appear to be the assaulter in that situation, but I am not. I am defending myself, using my experience to know that the guy is about to attack.

Balance is another example of *kyo*. If you can knock your opponent off balance with a sweep or something like that, then he is open. You also have mental *kyo*. This is where the opponent is off due to anger, fear, overexcitement, distraction.

If you deliver a technique from a weak platform, the technique is going to be weak. That is why we practice our stances, so we can deliver techniques with power.

Shotokan stances are long because we want to build up the legs. When you are looking at competition sparring, there may be a shorter stance when a technique is delivered, or it may be a longer stance, but are able to utilize either. You can take your pick.

Stances are used as transitions. You hit a stance for a second. It is the platform from which you deliver a technique or resist a force against you. Obviously, some stances are better suited for certain purposes than others.

There are two different kinds of stances: inside tension and outside tension. When you are in a stance, you are extremely stable. But if you are moving, or are on one leg, you are obviously unstable. Even if you are just moving from one position to another, or from one stance to another, you are unstable in that moment.

Stances are therefore very transitory. You should be hitting your stances at the moment of impact so you can resist the force against you and deliver whatever kinetic energy you are trying to deliver through whatever weapon you are using (hand, foot, etc.). This is why kicks are inherently unstable, since you are on one leg. You can mitigate this somewhat by bending your support leg to lower your center of gravity.

We always want to maintain a low center of gravity in our stances. We also want to maintain our line of gravity (typically by keeping our back straight). Stability depends on your base. The moment your center of gravity or line of gravity goes outside of your base, you are going to lose your balance. You are unstable.

The only leverage you have is the floor. If I could hang you from the ceiling by one hair, you would have little power. You would only have muscle contraction. It would not be an awful lot. But if I put you down on a solid surface, even if you could just lean against a wall, you would have leverage.

Typically, both of your feet are touching the floor. You should maximize your position on the floor to provide maximum leverage and power. Regardless of what power sources you are utilizing, such as rotation or momentum or vibration, basically all your leverage is from the floor. If your feet are slipping, it is because your center of gravity or your line of gravity has moved away from where it should be.

I like to get really low, and I like to move in really close. I do this because most people have longer legs than me, so I am at a disadvantage with an opponent who is strong at kicking. But if I can get in close, I can do some damage.

Some fighters are just natural athletes. They can adjust their stances and take the opportunity to drive in. But if you are going to drive in, you need pressure on that back leg. There is no other way to get momentum forward. Based on where your opponent positions their back leg, you can usually tell what they intend to do. You look at the way they are moving, try to pick up their rhythm, which is part of their breathing. Everything in life has a rhythm.

Many people do not understand rhythm when they are fighting. In my fighting days, I tended to do a lot of short techniques and then a long technique when the guy stops. Or I would back the guy into a corner, where psychologically he felt he had to do something. Then, as soon as he starts, you hit him. That is just tactics.

When I am assessing anybody in class or at a grading, I start from the feet up. If your feet are wrong, the rest of you is wrong. Also, I want students to align their joints correctly: shoulder, hip, knee, ankle. If you do not align correctly, you get a loss of connection.

When you make *kime* at the culmination of a technique, you want everything to be connected. If your shoulder is up, you are obviously disconnected from your lat muscle (latissimus dorsi, a large muscle in the back), so your hip is no longer involved, your lower body is no longer involved in the technique, so you are just throwing hands, which a lot of people do.

Excellent boxers such as Mike Tyson are always connected to the floor. Almost all his knockout punches came from a low to a high position. He was pushing up off the floor. It is the same in karate.

The basic muscle mechanism is contraction. Muscles only work by pulling, so you must get them into a position where they can pull. If you are in a front stance, your muscles cannot pull if the knee is not ahead of the ankle, so I am always saying, "Get your knee over your toe." And you start to move from your core (lower abdomen). The tendency is for people to lead with their shoulders or face. If you do that, you are pushing yourself into danger.

CHAPTER NINE

RESPECT

When I was growing up in England, it was very formal. Everybody wore shirts and ties. I am wearing a shirt and tie in my Seaman's Book, from when I was in the Merchant Navy. I was never called by my first name until I came to Canada. I was always referred to as Mr. Hanratty. I was quite surprised when I came to Canada and people were saying, "Hey, John." I'm thinking, "Who are you talking to? A little bit of respect, please."

Everybody did that in England. They were formal, but they were friendly. If people used your first name, they had to be close friends. It was the same in the Army. You were always called by your surname, never by anything else.

I try to instill in my students a respect for other people. The important of this is obvious if you are sparring with a partner, so you do not hurt them. In the dojo and on the street, never underestimate anybody else. Consider everyone to be at least your equal, until proved otherwise. Respect everybody else because everyone is trying to get through life. We are all trying to get by. Life is very short. How you fill it is up to you.

Karate-do aims to foster harmony among people, with *rei* (courtesy) as its foundational element in achieving human harmony. This value of courtesy is a core tenet in all *budo*, hence the maxim: "*Budo* starts with courtesy and ends with courtesy." In modern terms, "courtesy" is often replaced with "politeness," a term more familiar to many students. Generally, politeness begets politeness. When politeness is not returned, a person's weaknesses and shortcomings are more apparent, leaving them vulnerable to defeat.

Kids will sometimes wait outside the dojo after class and say, "May I ask you a question?" Just the fact they say, "May I ask you a question?" is good because already we have started to bring in some manners, some discipline, some respect. I try to instill that respect by always referring to my black belts as "Mr." I try to get that across to the students.

A sign of too much ego is when you see bullying in sparring. I have shut people down hard for that. Mouthing off is another sign. I watch for lack of respect shown to their partner, especially if it is a lower grade they are working with; in some cases, if it is a different sex. We have had people who bullied women and I have thrown them out of the club. You will often hear me walking down the line saying, "Use control, use control."

We always recite the *dojo kun* at the end of the class. They are the basic rules we go by. They encourage respect for yourself and others. We recite them in Japanese. Some clubs choose to recite them in English.

Seek perfection of character
Jinkaku kansei ni tsutomuru koto

Be faithful
Makoto no michi o mamoru koto

Endeavour
Doryoku no seishin o yashinau koto

Respect others
Reigi o omonzuru koto

Refrain from violent behaviour
Keki no yu o imashimuru koto

The unique sense of camaraderie found in a karate club can only be appreciated through attendance. Your current fitness level and your natural physical ability does not matter. So long as you show up and make an effort, and are respectful of the other students, you are going to be supported and encouraged to get better. There is an instant acceptance. There is a special connection you feel when you work hard with a group of other people.

When students come into class, I like to feel that I take all their daily worries off them. I fill their minds with other stuff. You cannot be thinking, "I wonder what's for dinner?" when somebody is trying to punch your head off. You cannot be worrying about your bank balance when I am screaming at you to get your stance lower and to make sure your weight is evenly distributed and that your hips are underneath you. All you can think about is what you are doing and how you can do it better. When the time is finished and you bow out, hopefully it has refreshed you.

You rarely get bullies coming into a karate club. People who just want to dominate others do not last very long. The discipline will usually sort them out. If not, we have people who have been through it all and know what to look for. I have thrown people out of the club after five or ten minutes. I have no problem with that.

I have kicked a black belt out of the club for not respecting other students, for hurting them. I kicked another one out for drug use. I cannot have anybody in my dojo who does drugs. Tragically, a few years later the drug user was found dead in his home. Someone had shot him.

Karate students are on the road to improvement of character. I refuse to say perfection of character, because you cannot perfect it. But hopefully you can improve it. And while you can enhance your character through karate, it is not the only way, of course. If you do something well enough, it is going to improve your character, so long as it is within the law. It is an educational process. If you are not looking at it that way, you are going at it the wrong way. It is not just a physical pursuit, because the physical component diminishes as you get older. And getting old is tough. It is not for wimps.

When I first started training, you could not question anything. You worked your heart out. You might just do kicks or punches or blocks all night, and you could not question why you were doing them. Now, I have a different philosophy. I explain to you why you are doing it and why it works, but we could not do that at the Triangle. We just sweated away and worked away. Then we all went out the door and disappeared until next time. I did not know where a lot of those guys lived, but I wanted to return for that feeling of cohesiveness, that camaraderie.

Karate interested me from the start. It was exotic. But that disappears straight away. You have your little rituals. That is your first introduction to self discipline. I love *mokuso*, where you close your eyes and breathe at the end of the class. By that time, your mind is clear. You are just glad your struggle to perform the techniques is over. Sweat is usually dripping off you and your body is tired and sore. And you just take some deep breaths and relax.

Karate was a form of meditation for me. It was moving Zen. This concept is discussed in a great book by C.W. Nicol called *Moving Zen*. Zen is about living in the moment. That is what you are doing in karate. It is like taking your mind to the drycleaners. Poof – fresh when you come out. That is what I loved about karate when I first started training. Nothing could intrude because you are concentrating so much on what you are doing. There were no other worries. It was just work, work, work, and your mind emptied. You are concentrating on what you are doing in the moment.

I try to get this across to my students: you should be involved in the moment. We refer to the state of awareness in the present moment as *zanshin*. I have had some students with me for 10 or 12 years who still do not get that. Every now and then, you will see them get it, but not a lot of them. They are looking for something else, something that is easier.

CHAPTER TEN

SPIRIT

You must train with spirit. Your spirit must be controlled aggression. Karate is controlled violence. There is no other way to really describe it.

Spirit is a motivation, a desire. It is a desire to perfect what you are trying to do, or at least to do it as well as you can. If you have a desire to do better, you will progress. My job is to motivate you and ignite that desire.

The only thing I want from the mental side, particularly with beginners, is spirit. I do my best to develop their spirit, their interest, their desire, and their enthusiasm. It is all part of spirit, as far as I am concerned. If I can develop that, they are going to want more and more and more, and that "wanting more" is probably the best thing a teacher can encourage.

You need to keep your aggression in check so that your adrenaline does not take over. Adrenaline is a very useful hormone. It gives you a fight-or-flight response that can either save you or kill you. It gives you the adrenaline to run away or to fight for your life. But it is a bugger of a hormone because it is slow to come on, but when it does, it over dumps. It is very hard to control. I have experienced this: your vision tends to tunnel, your mouth will dry out because all the blood is pulled into the internal organs to protect them, and all your fine motor skills go out the window.

I was once in a bad argument with a Japanese instructor in British Columbia. He practiced a different style and he was kind of drunk. He was threatening me. I was trying not to get mad. He thought his karate was superior, but it was a load of crap. It was a great exercise in adrenaline control for me because I just wanted to pound him and I knew I could, but he did not know I could. If I had not learned to control my response to adrenaline, there could have been a bad outcome.

I have been in enough street fights to know that adrenaline will get you in more trouble than not, where you just want to go at somebody, and in a street fight you do not have to worry about rules. Standard procedure for a street fight is eye jab, headbutt, knee strike, elbow strikes. As many as you can in as short a time, then get yourself home.

My talent as a street fighter and survivalist was attacking the intention. Attacking the intention may sound a bit barbaric and it may look as though I am attacking the other guy, but if I have noticed that his intention is not exactly honourable, or if his intent is violence, all I do is pre-empt that by attacking his intention. It gets a person out of so much trouble.

In hockey and other sports, it is often said that the best defence is a good offence. This is true in karate as well. Attacking the intention does not make you the aggressor. It just means you recognize that the intention to harm you typically appears before any physical action by the other person.

In the dojo, you need to bring out the best you have in yourself. This is the whole object of training. If you ever need it, you must be the best you can be in that moment. You cannot throw a half-hearted technique if you are defending yourself. It must be the very best that you have.

Many outside variables will try to pull you away from giving your best. These variables include psychological pressure, adrenaline dump, and fear of injury (especially if someone has a weapon). Even if you only deliver 60 per cent of your best because of these variables, it must be sufficient. You must let go of any fear and just let your spirit out.

CHAPTER ELEVEN

COMPETITION

Competition is good. If you can develop a good competitive atmosphere in an organization, that organization will grow, because people will enjoy attending and they will have a more definite goal in mind than just collecting belts.

Competition plays a big role for little kids if you let it. I am not a believer in participation trophies. I have had a few people come up to me at a competition and go, "Well, can you give a fourth-place medal?" My answer is always no. If it was up to me, there would be only one winner. That is the way the world works. Face it, we are humans, we are animals. It is survival of the fittest.

In my competition days, I never liked earning a silver medal. No matter how many fights preceded the final match, in the final match there are only two of you. There is a winner and a loser. A silver medal means you lost.

Competitiveness was part of my growing up. You had to compete. This is instinctive, especially in a bad environment. Survival is an instinct. Competition and games that you play as a kid develop that, so you can survive your surroundings. Everybody I knew as a kid was trying to be good at something, trying to be better than another kid at something. You do not get that as much these days.

That mentality came from the survival of the fittest and the times. It was probably even worse as you look back through history. People had to do all sorts of things to survive. It has gotten easier and easier. Nowadays, competition is not even encouraged, which is silly because it is an ingrained thing with most people. Whether you do it consciously or not, you want to get to where you are going, despite the people and circumstances that get in your way.

Kids today seem softer, especially when I think of the conditions of my upbringing. With some of my students, I go, "Okay when you get into a street fight…" and they say, "I've never been in a street fight, ever." I have been in street fights as far back as I can remember, and this is the everyday experience for people in many parts of the world.

In England, you could not compete until you were a green belt. The competitions were entirely different than in North America. When you entered a competition, there were no weights, no heights, and no ranks. Your name was drawn out of a hat, and you fought who you fought.

I was about 27 the first time I entered a competition. I had been training for two years and had my green belt. I got drawn up against Bobby Poynton, who was the European champion at the time. He was a 4th Dan. We were good friends at the time and remained close for the rest of his life. I am not sure if it was accidental or not, but I got a punch in on him, earning the first half-point. That was the last thing I remember, because then he absolutely finished me off. He had telescopic legs and was a good six or eight inches taller than me.

I was laughing afterward. I was not nervous before or during the fight because it was not a fight-fight. I have been in fights where you had to bite the guy's face off to get home. This was not a fight; this was a competition. There were rules. The most I would get is a black eye or a split lip. I have never been scared in competition. There is nothing to fear.

Modern karate tries to build interest by doing loads of competitions. Which is not karate; it is competition. A whole different thing.

I always enjoyed participating in competitions. My problem was, when it came to the *kumite* section, it was more attitude than technique. I would just go at my opponent, and you could tell I was seriously going to hurt somebody. That held me back a lot on gradings. I guess I intimidated people, even though I was smaller and lighter than most of them. If you have a bit of confidence, it tends to come out in such situations.

In 1989, I won the first Masters competition ever held in Canada. That year I also won Coach of the Year and was nominated for Canada Sportsman of the Year. Our Alberta team won a whole bunch of medals that year. I knew I would not win Sportsman of the Year because I was up against hockey players. I think Ben Johnson (an Olympic runner) was also nominated.

I was in my 40s when I competed in the Masters, and you only had to be 35 to get into the Masters, so I was probably always the oldest competitor. I was awarded first in *kumite* and second in *kata*, and that happened two years in a row. I could never get first in *kata*. Some competitors only did *kata*. The guy who won the kata, I had never seen him compete in *kumite*.

I was 50 when I won the North American Masters, held in California. I got first in *kumite* and second in *kata*, again. I had 12 fights in a row and the final fight was against a guy called Jim Hawkins who was a pretty good fighter. The refereeing was tough – you could not buy a point. You had to practically knock the guy out to get a point. I came off the floor after the fight full of lumps and bruises. I took three Tylenol and promptly fell asleep on the bench until they announced the winners. Then I went up and got my trophy.

I did not know at the time that it would be my last competition. In fact, I was planning to compete the next year. A couple of the guys came up to me beforehand and said, "Are you going in?" I said, "I'm thinking of it." One of them said, "Well, if you're going in, I'm not." I thought, "Oh, okay, I won't."

Part of my reasoning was that, at age 50, I did not particularly want to risk injury. It was very hard to earn a point in that competition unless you really hit the guy. And I could sense that the other competitors, all of whom were younger than me, were out for revenge. I also knew that if I got hurt, I would beat the hell out of anyone they put in front of me. I would do my best to, anyway. The rules would be out the window at that point.

When it comes to running a competition, basically you want to see who has the best-trained people. That is what it is for. Everybody wants to prove how well they have been training, to see if their techniques work, along with their timing, distance, flexibility, and so on.

All these elements are included in the criteria for judging. The criteria for judging *kumite* are all laid out: technique, direction, speed; likewise for *kata*: eye direction, balance, and so on. What you must do to win and what the judges should be looking for when it comes to the different points is in the rulebooks. But it is just for points – you are not allowed to pound the guy. It is like the joke about the guy in the street who is supposedly a world champion. The other guy is pounding his face in and he is going, "I tapped out, I tapped out!" A competition is very different from real life.

A truly engaging competition is one that is both exciting to watch and to participate in. Generally, contests that captivate spectators also provide a thrilling experience for competitors. Everybody likes a crowd and enjoys the chance to prove to everybody, "Hey, I'm good at this." You can spar in the dojo, which has its merits, but it lacks the exhilaration of performing in front of a large audience.

If you run a competition, and I have run a lot of competitions, you want to make it exciting for the people there. When doing the draws, try to get the biggest variation you can at the start, so nobody fights anybody from their own club. When I organized the first Nationals in Calgary in 1984, I brought in an international team to compete. Sensei Masami Tsuruoka and a few others did not like it. They said, "Oh no, this is the *Canadian* black belt championships." I said, "Yeah, but it's a demonstration. People pay to see a demonstration." It worked. We filled the gym at the university hosting the event.

The most exciting part of most competitions is team *kumite* because you get behind a team. Sometimes you can get behind an individual, but if he is on a team, you are going to get behind him even more, and then you get behind his team. Therefore, you always want a team event, if possible, especially team *kumite*. It gets the crowd up, it gets the competitors up, and it makes the referees a bit sharper.

For a good competition you need good referees. When I run referee courses, I am rather strict on what you can and cannot get away with. You must be consistent. Consistency in officiating is the backbone of competition. Still, you are going to get personalities involved. There are idiosyncrasies. What may constitute excessive or bad in one person's mind may not be in the other person's mind, except when it is absolutely obvious.

Where you come across politics the most is in officiating, and it spoils a lot of competition. But if you make the guidelines too strict, there is no point in having an official. There is always a gray area that is going to be subjective. There are going to be personal preferences.

If it was up to me, we would never use pads, including fist pads, and we would never use mats. Mats, in my opinion, are dangerous. It is very hard to spin quickly on a mat and I have seen people twist their ankle and tear ligaments. One fighter of mine in Liverpool, in 2013, badly ripped his hamstring. It absolutely finished his karate training. Took the tendon right off the bone. He got stuck on the mat as he went forward on a kick.

When I am training referees, the main point is the safety of the athletes. That is number one. That is what you are there for. Make sure nobody goes outside the rules and make sure that any points that you award are within the criteria for that technique. And it is all written down. It is not hard.

You must be obvious, so we use these big hand signals. They cannot hear you in the stands if you are in a big competition, so the hand signals convey your decision regarding a point or a penalty or whatever. And the penalties are nearly all for the safety of the athletes. They are not to give the other guy a point. A penalty is not for the benefit of the guy getting hit. First, you should ask yourself, "Should he have blocked that?" And then, "Did this guy hit with intent to control or not?"

As a referee, you must show confidence. As soon as you take control of that ring, the athletes must have confidence in you. Once they have confidence in you, they will trust you to make the right decisions. You must be firm.

I had an argument in Hungary a few years ago. The chief referee came barging into my ring, and I threw him out. He started to argue with me. I said, "Okay, hang on, then you take it. I'm out of here." And he backed right down. You do not come into my ring.

Often, little kids will throw a punch and it will be maybe two inches away from their opponent and the referee will go, "No point." So, the next punch they throw is an inch away, and he goes, "No point." So, they hit their opponent with their next punch, and they get disqualified. That is so stupid. If it was an inch away, and the other kid never blocked, you must give the point. These are kids you are talking about. You cannot mess around. If you do not give the point, they are going to try harder and harder. You are going to end up with an accident, and you know what? It will be the referee's fault.

One of the best fights I ever saw was Steve Cattle and Terry O'Neill in 1977 or 1978 at Crystal Palace. That year, I got through to the last 16 and came up against the European champion, George

Godfrey. He was 6'3". I have pictures of me fighting him and I look like a midget going up against King Kong.

At the Crystal Palace you fight all day and there are something like twenty areas that you fight in. If you win in one area, you take your ticket and go to another area. It is single elimination. Then the finals are in the evening – the final four.

After my final fight, I got changed and went to watch the other fights. Terry O'Neill was fighting Phil Duvall in the semi-final, and they are having a good go. Phil was a big kid. Terry does a *ushiro-geri* (spinning back kick) and Phil goes to block down, with a double-hand block, and Terry switches it to a *ura-mawashi geri* (hook kick). Caught him right in the head with his heel. Phil hits the floor. He is out cold. Sensei Enoeda gives *ippon* (full point) to Terry.

Enoeda then brings in the judges to confer. Enoeda's ruling is that Terry's kick did not knock Phil out, it was hitting his head on the floor that knocked him out, so Terry gets the point. Now, I am not saying politics was involved or not, but it was a beautiful kick, so I would have been sad if Terry had been disqualified. That was not the way that the KUGB worked, or the way JKA fighting worked. You did a kick like that, you got a point.

In the next match, Terry came up against Steve Cattle. This was the final. Steve was a famous fighter, an ex-member of the UK judo team. He was a lovely man but a really fierce fighter. His strategy was getting in close, while Terry was more of a kicker.

They were drawn at the end of the match, so it went into overtime. At that time there was no limit on the number of overtimes. You fought until you had a winner, especially in a final. Finals were three minutes long, and these guys had been fighting in previous fights as well. It ended up going to three overtimes.

In the final overtime, Terry tried something I had never seen anybody do. He throws a *kizami* punch (lead hand punch), dives into a forward roll, brings his foot up behind him, and with his heel catches Steve right in the middle of the chest as Steve is trying to punch. He got an *ippon* for that, and that was a win. That was a brilliant fight. Best fight I have ever seen.

In a competition, you are generally thinking about attacking. Not many people throw *mawashi geri* (roundhouse kick) in defence. You can maybe throw *gyaku-zuki* (reverse punch) but you need pick up a rhythm to do that. That is really, really important, and it is hard to teach a rhythm, because when you are looking at attack and defence, if you tell two students, "You're the attacker and you're the defender," who will be the most on edge? The defender is always on edge because the attacker knows what he is doing.

If I put somebody in front of you and say, "He's going to attack you with *oi-zuke* (lead hand punch)," which is generally a slow technique, you are ready to move before the attacker does anything. As the defender, you should just relax and observe the rhythm of the attacker's breathing. Something will happen before he starts. You can pick up on that.

I try to teach this in basics when students are doing one-step drills. It is hard to get it across to many people, and if you are just doing sport karate, they do not teach that. They do not teach basics. They go straight into, "This is *mawashi-geri*, this is *ura-mawashi*," because they are the high-point techniques.

There is a myth that says there is competition karate and then there is traditional karate. This is nonsense, because most so-called traditional organizations, such as the KUGB, do competitions almost every month. The role of competition is good, but right now it just validates what people are training for. The problem is, they are training only for competition. They are not training for self-defence or a way of life, which is what karate-do is — a way of life that will help you throughout your life.

My main beef with sport karate is that it is very short lived. Your competitive life is relatively short. I mean, look at soccer players – they get paid millions, but they are all done at 35. They might get a job as a manager, but that is only four or five per cent of them. The rest of them are done. It is the same in any sport. It is short-lived. Consider the UFC (Ultimate Fighting Championship). You do not see guys my age doing UFC or even martial arts such as jujitsu. Competition is a young man's game.

I am probably a little biased about sport karate because I started late. If I had started at 12 or 14, maybe I would be a little more favourable in my competitive attitude. With the instructors I have trained with, and I have trained with just about any high-grade instructor you can name, their philosophy has not leaned toward the competitive side. What they will do is show you the techniques – how to do them, how to build power, how to build speed – and then you can use them in competition. But you are not going to get a lot out of a competitive fighter if you throw them into the street. I can think of maybe two or three times that I have thrown a perfect technique in the street. Most of it has been sheer bloody-mindedness – an "I'm gonna rip your face off" kind of deal.

A typical competitive fighter does not have experience in the kind of adrenaline you get in a street fight. You do get a certain adrenaline rush when competing, mind you. Do not get me wrong: I loved it. When I competed, I got a bit of a rush from it. You would review your competition fights in your mind afterward. But it is not unusual to go over your street fights in your mind for six or seven months afterward. It is just such an adrenaline rush.

The role of the adrenaline rush is discussed in a book about the psychology behind football hooliganism called *The Football Factory*, by John King. They get such a rush from hooliganism, the edge of danger, that it becomes addictive.

I used to get adrenaline rushes from skydiving. I did a bunch of skydiving in my 20s, after my stint in the Army. I loved the feeling, the sheer rush of going out. We were thrown out at the end of a static line. We used old military chutes. You would hook your static line to where they took the seats out, with a U-clamp. You would jump out, and your static line was maybe 20 feet long and it opened your chute.

You had a static line for your first three or four jumps, and then it was up to you to pull your ripcord. The most apprehensive jump was the first one where I had to pull it myself, because I'm thinking, "Okay, if I don't pull this, I'm going to plunge to the ground."

The first bunch of times you jump, everything happens in an instant and you are suddenly down on the ground. Over time, your mind kind of catches up to the speed your body is moving, and you can do a lot while falling. On your first 30-second freefall, you are doing left and right turns and backflips. You had to learn different maneuvers before you got your various licenses. You also earned a packing certificate, and a rigging certificate, so you knew how to repair stuff.

I have always had a tough time being afraid of anything, even death. There were times when I was at sea as a young man in a force-10 gale and the ship was rolling like crazy and I was unphased. What is going to happen is going to happen. Mortality does not bother me at all. I am at peace with it.

You can refer almost any situation in life to a karate situation or principle, to help you deal with it. This is also true of other philosophical viewpoints such as stoicism or whatever – you can refer any situation to a philosophy that suits your particular mindset and it will work, it will fit.

I am a big believer in karate as a way of life. At the same time, if you want to just use it as recreation, or fitness, or self defence, it is there for you. Getting people to invest in karate as a way of life is extremely difficult. It does not come immediately. It comes slowly, after they get used to doing it. They eventually see the benefits of it and want to go more in-depth.

CHAPTER TWELVE

REFLECTION

Coming from a city like Liverpool in those post-war years, when it was dealing with unemployment, poverty, and many other challenges, it would have been easy to go in a different direction. And many of our people did turn out bad. For me and many others, the natural instinct to compete, the natural motivation to always push yourself ahead, could easily turn in another direction and you ended up as a gangster or something.

As I often say, life is about choices. The choices you made in the past made you who you are today.

As far back as I can remember, I have had a strong sense of who I am and what is important to me. A few times I have thought, "I've taken too much on" and I have felt a little bit like an imposter at times, especially as I got up in higher grades. But then people go, "Look at what you've done. You've done this and this and this and this." I never looked back on past things to support where I was. I just accepted it.

Sometimes I would be standing in a line with karate students bowing in, there would be 300 people facing me, and I would think, "I'm going to be teaching these people in an hour – I feel like an imposter." But then you do it and they say, "Fantastic class!" and you are like, "Oh, thank you."

I certainly miss being as fit as I used to be. I do not know how it would go if I had to use martial arts now. One thing is for sure: I would not back down. It is just not in me. I might be too old to fight, but I am definitely too old to lose a fight.

Karate has given me an awful lot. Not just because I have been able to travel with it, or compete with it, or get the odd accolade here and there. That is not what it is about. What it has done, I think, is made me a better person. And whether I have taught people for a month, a year, or 30 years, hopefully it has done the same for them.

Karate is very much a self-sacrificing thing, but it is also self-satisfying. I do not believe anybody in this world ever does anything that does not have a selfish aspect to some extent. I mean, if you give money to the poor, part of the reason you give is because it makes you feel good. It is like that with karate. You do what makes you feel good, and at my stage I am giving back because it makes me feel good to give back and to bring people along. I do my best to ensure they are on the right path.

Besides karate, I have had a very full life. Having traveled all around the world before I was 18, I had many varied experiences. My time in the Army and coming from probably one of the toughest cities in the world, that all pushes you into the persona you have, not just karate. If anything, I think karate mellowed me. It took stuff that I could have gone wrong with and channeled it in a good way.

I do not know what my legacy will be. At my age, I have had many friends pass away, and you try to remember little bits about them. Everybody has a different meaning or a different point of view on what you are trying to put across. I just hope that people will say, "Well, he was a pretty good guy." That's it. I am not really worried about them saying, "He was fantastic at karate."

There are a lot of people I admire in the karate world and elsewhere. You admire people for what they have done. I believe you can never judge a person's motives, only their actions. You do not really know their motives. Hopefully they are pure. Some of them turn out not to be. All you can do is shrug your shoulders and move on.

I have only a few photos and videos of myself. Sometimes I wish I had more. But that is just not me. Self promotion comes more naturally to some people than others. When I was in my mid-60s, I was at a karate camp to teach and they had mats down, and I dove into a forward roll. One of the guys said, "Wow, can you do that again? I've never seen anyone your age do that." I said, "No, sod off." I could have, but I was not there to show off.

I did okay at karate when I was younger. I am certainly not doing karate as well now, but I am still teaching. I still have a lot to teach, and I know when former students come back there is a great deal of respect. I can feel that. A guy who was on the national team years ago came into the dojo recently with his daughter. He was over the moon to come back and smell the dojo and see the people in their *gis*. I may not be around to teach forever, but we have a good dojo and it is a bit of a legacy.

My philosophy in life is to find one thing that you love and do it. Now, if you are really lucky, what you love will also be how you earn a living. Karate was never how I earned a living, but it was what I loved. I believe if you put all your energy into doing what you love, it will richly reward you. I always worked first for my family but, secondly, I worked so I could do karate.

I never lived for work; I worked so I could live. I believe that is the way you should do it. You need to balance it out. If you find yourself thinking, "I wish I'd spent more time with my family," it tells me you lacked balance. You are probably looking at some parts of your life as a failure. You should be at peace with what you are doing and who you are. That is going to be a better life for you in the long run. I am totally at peace with who I am and what I have done.

I know I have made an impression on some people. It is like footprints in the sand. If you leave a footprint in the sand, you are probably doing more with your life than some people. The waves are going to eventually wash it away, and a hundred years from now nobody will know anything about it, but that is okay.

I am proud of the fact that I am still going in my late 70s. I am still hitting the gym and still training a few times a week. I am happy with that. I have a different philosophy on life and death than many others. I have no idea what people will remember me by. But I hope they remember me fondly.

When I do eventually go, I want it to be sudden. And I want it to be in a dojo. That's it, just bang! Gone. Right in the middle of *Bassai-dai* or something.